Success in Literacy Reading Tests

UNDERSTANDING
▨ YEAR 5
COMPREHENSION
Excellent for all Students, Teachers, Coaches and Parents

Authors

Alan Horsfield   M.Ed., B.A., B.Ed., Dip.Sch.Admin., TESOL, Teaching Cert.
Alan Horsfield has more than 35 years teaching experience in state and private schools in New South Wales and International Schools in Papua New Guinea. He was employed by UNSW (EAA) as an English Research Officer involved in the construction of school tests for English and Mathematics. Alan is a published writer of children's fiction, educational material and school texts.

Elaine Horsfield   M.A. (Theatre Studies), B.A. (Theatre Media), Teaching Cert.
Elaine Horsfield has more than 25 years teaching experience in Primary Schools both with the New South Wales Department of Education and in International Schools in Papua New Guinea. She worked with secondary students as coordinator of the NSW Talent Development Project. Elaine is a published writer of children's poetry and educational books.

Editor:
Warwick Marlin B.Sc. Dip.Ed.

Publisher:
Five Senses Education
ABN: 16 001 414437
2/195 Prospect Highway
Seven Hills NSW Australia 2147
sevenhills@fivesenseseducation.com.au
www.fivesenseseducation.com.au

Trade Enquiries:
Phone (02) 9838 9265
Fax (02) 9838 8982
Email: fsonline@fivesenseseducation.com.au

Understanding Year 5 Comprehension
ISBN: 978-1-76032-019-5
1st **Edition:** July 2014
Copyright: Alan Horsfield © Five Senses Education Pty. Ltd. © Warwick Marlin

AUTHOR'S ACKNOWLEDGEMENTS

Warwick Marlin, my editor, whose advice and guidance have been very much appreciated.

Roger Furniss, at Five Senses Education for publishing my books.

And above all, to **Jones**, my typesetter, for a high standard of typesetting, layout and artwork. A very special thank you for your time, patience, attention to detail, and overall quality of your work.

PARENTS

This book tells you what the teacher often does not have the time to explain in detail - the intricacies of a wide variation in text types and the testing strategies used by Australian testing institutions to asses progress in Literacy. It will give you confidence to support your children by reinforcing what is being taught in schools and what is being tested, especially Reading Comprehension.

TEACHERS

This book introduces text types and test question types Australian students should understand to maximise internal and external Reading Tests. Reading tests may involve comprehension as well as related grammar questions. It eliminates the need to wade through lengthy curriculum documents and it provides a clear and easy to follow format for teachers to use. Teachers can also confidently recommend this book to parents as it supports classroom activities and exercises.

B. Ed., Dip. Ed. PRIMARY SCHOOL TEACHERS

This book contains a variety of recognised primary school text types with question sets that will improve reading comprehension and improved results in reading tests. It acts as a quick reference book for teachers in the early years of teaching, when there is so much to learn.

Understanding Year 5 Comprehension
A. Horsfield © Five Senses Education © W. Marlin

AVAILABILITY OF MATHEMATICS BOOKS

All of the Mathematics books below have been produced by the same editor and publisher, and in many cases the same author (Warwick Marlin). Therefore they all incorporate the same high presentation and philosophy. They can be purchased directly from Five Senses Education, but they are also available in most educational bookshops throughout NSW and Australia (and also some selected bookshops in New Zealand).

New National Curriculum titles

The eight school titles listed directly below have been rewritten and updated in recent years to closely follow the New National Curriculum. **'All levels'** means that the books have been written for students of most ability groups (weak, average and gifted). The graded tests at the end of each chapter ensure that students of most ability groups are extended to their full potential.

❑	YEAR 1	ALL LEVELS
❑	YEAR 2	ALL LEVELS
❑	YEAR 3	ALL LEVELS
❑	YEAR 4	ALL LEVELS
❑	YEAR 5	ALL LEVELS
❑	YEAR 6	ALL LEVELS
❑	YEAR 7	ALL LEVELS
❑	YEAR 8	ALL LEVELS

Other titles in this series

The titles listed below are also available, but they will be fully updated during 2014 and 2015 to also closely follow the new curriculum. However, in the meantime, please note, that these books still adequately address the main features of the new syllabus. We firmly believe that the major topics explained in these titles, and our user friendly presentation and development of the different topics, will always continue to form the vital foundations for all future study and applications of mathematics. This is especially so for the titles up to, and including, Year 10 Advanced.

❑	YEAR 9 & 10	INTERMEDIATE
❑	YEAR 9 & 10	ADVANCED
❑	YEAR 11 & 12	GENERAL MATHS
❑	YEAR 11	EXTENSION 1
❑	YEAR 12	EXTENSION 1

Also by the same Author and Editor (Warwick Marlin)

❑	ESSENTIAL EXERCISES YEAR 1	ALL LEVELS
❑	ESSENTIAL EXERCISES YEAR 2	ALL LEVELS
❑	ESSENTIAL EXERCISES YEAR 3	ALL LEVELS
❑	ESSENTIAL EXERCISES YEAR 4	ALL LEVELS
❑	ESSENTIAL EXERCISES YEAR 5	ALL LEVELS
❑	ESSENTIAL EXERCISES YEAR 6	ALL LEVELS

Developed & written in 2012, this excellent new series of books closely follows the Australian National Curriculum.

CONTENTS

Page

INTRODUCTION

- Acknowledgments iii

- Availability of books by the same editor & publisher iv

- Understanding Year 5 English Testing vi

- How to use this book effectively vii

- Test sources viii

- A brief summary of some question formats ix

- A practice test x

Year 5 Comprehension Passages and Exercises

These tests include narratives, poems, procedures, recounts, explanations, descriptions, cartoons and reports. At the end of each test there is also a valuable and well explained literacy tip. 1

ANSWERS - Reading Comprehension Tests 83, 84

ANSWERS - Literacy Tip Exercises 85, 86

"So it is with children who learn to read fluently and well. They begin to take flight into whole new worlds as effortlessly as young birds take to the sky."

William James

Understanding Year 5 Comprehension
A. Horsfield © Five Senses Education © W. Marlin

UNDERSTANDING YEAR 5 ENGLISH TESTING

This is an important year in the child's education. Year 5 is a NAPLAN testing year. Groundwork commenced in the earlier years leads to a more formal development of literacy understanding. It is a time when the school and the home continue to work closely together. It is important that the home has a positive attitude to school and education, and also provides support with an abundance of practical activities in an environment that stimulates curiosity and enjoyment in reading and writing. The more literacy experiences the child has, the more realistic and practical will be the child's foundation in literacy in later years, and the more confidence the child will have.

Through the later primary years the student continues to move from literal comprehension of text to the more abstract. What is implied becomes more and more important. This transition will vary from child to child. At times, we all read different 'messages' into text. It is also important to understand that we don't necessarily grasp the intended meaning on a first reading. Re-reading is an important strategy.

Remember: Do not have unreal expectations of what your child can read. Don't 'push' too hard, especially with the more formal written work. Keep literacy fun, especially in reading and then attitudes will be positive. At times it is fun to read something that is not so challenging!

The best way to succeed in any test is to practice.
An old Chinese proverb sums it up well:
> I hear, I forget;
> I see, I remember;
> I do, I understand.

I enjoy a little bit of recreational reading every day!

The NAPLAN testing program for Australian Schools treats three strands of English.
Reading tests, which include the comprehension of a variety of text types,
Writing tests, which focus on writing a narrative, a persuasive text or a recount,
Language Conventions tests, which include Spelling, Punctuation and Grammar.

All three strands are interrelated in the 'real world'. As the National Curriculum states, "Teaching and learning programs should balance and integrate all three strands"
(see:http://www.australiancurriculum.edu.au/Year5).The 'interpretation' of digital text becomes increasingly important and relevant.

This book is based on Year levels not Stages. (There are three basic primary school stages. Year 5 and Year 6 make up Stage 3*. In Year 5 there is a strong emphasis on comprehending a variety of text types of increasing difficulty and subtlety. Not all text types get the same attention. The study of persuasive text is more complex and subtle than, say, following directions. As families and society are a complex mix of differing experiences, children will have different exposure to different text types. Individual children will develop different strengths and weaknesses.

This book focuses specifically on Reading but the skills learned in Reading can assist in the development of the child's Writing skills. The skills learned in the Language Convention strand can improve both Reading and Writing.

That is why we have included a Literacy Tip (**Lit Tip**) component at the end of each set of questions. These may help with any Language Convention questions that come up in standardised reading tests as well adding 'tricks' that may improve the quality of Writing test responses.

HOW TO USE THIS BOOK EFFECTIVELY

As stated, this book's primary aim is to improve Reading comprehension with some input into Language Conventions. Obviously the Speaking, Listening and Handwriting strands are not included.

The passages are not selected in any specific order but are intended to present a wide variation of text types. Those most likely to be part of the testing situation are treated more often. The text type is shown at the top of each passage as well as in the **List of comprehension passages and exercises** chart that follows.

There will be differences of focus from school to school, as teachers tend to select topics in varying sequences according to their program at a particular time in the year. Some students may also be involved in accelerated promotion, enrichment or remedial activities

ABOUT THE EXERCISES

The intent of the 40 passages is to provide one passage per week for each school week. This should not impinge too much on obligations set by the school/class teacher for homework and research. There is one easier **practice passage** provided to make the child aware of a range of question types that may be encountered.
Children need not work through the exercisers from 1 to 40 in the order in which they are presented in this book. There is the option of practicing a particular text type, e.g. poetry.

The Comprehension Answers and the Lit Tip Answers are on separate pages at the back of the book.

Reading texts can be based on either **Factual** or **Literary** texts.
Year 5 question types often include the skills of:

- **Locating** such things as information, a sequence of events, literary techniques, grammar conventions and vocabulary features.

- **Identifying** genres, the purpose of a text, literary techniques, appropriate punctuation, word meanings.

- **Interpreting** visual information, multiple pieces of information, language style.

- **Inferring** next events in a text, reasons for a character's action, outcomes, the effect of tense and person.

- **Synthesising** the tone of a text, the main idea in a text, a character's motivation, the writer's opinion, the intended audience for a text.

These above skills are more or less arranged in an order of difficulty.

Alan Horsfield M.Ed., B.A., B.Ed., Dip.Sch.Admin., TESOL, Teaching Cert.
Elaine Horsfield M. A. (Theatre Studies), B. A. (Theatre Media), Teaching Cert.

Understanding Year 5 Comprehension
A. Horsfield © Five Senses Education © W. Marlin

TEST SOURCES

The questions, information and practice provided by this book will benefit the student sitting for the following tests.

Externally produced tests

> NAPLAN (National Assessment - Literacy and Numeracy) Used Australia wide.
> PAT (-R) (Progressive Achievements Tests - Reading)
> ICAS (International Competitions and Assessments for Schools) Run by EAA.
> Selective Schools and High Schools Placement Tests (Most states have tests specific to that state's educational policy.)
> Scholarship Tests
> ACER (Australian Council for Educational Research) Scholarship tests (Most states have tests specific to that state's educational policy)
> AusVELS (Australian Curriculum in Victoria Essential Learning Standards)
> Independent Assessment Agencies (e.g. Academic Assessment Services)
> ISA (International Schools Assessment) run by ACER

There may be a number of other independent, external sources for literacy testing.

School produced tests

- year tests
- class tests
- school tests

Information provided in this book may also be beneficial in certain competitions run by commercial enterprises.

A number of commercial publishers also provide books of practice tests.

The purpose of testing

Testing has a variety of purposes and the purpose will often determine the type of test administered. Tests may be used to:
- determine what the student has learned
- rank students in order of ability
- select the most worthy students for a school or class
- determine the strength and weakness of classroom teaching
- determine any 'short-comings' in a school's educational program
- ascertain the effectiveness of certain teaching strategies
- evaluate the effectiveness of departmental/official syllabuses

A BRIEF SUMMARY OF SOME QUESTION FORMATS

Look at the nursery rhyme, **Mary had a Little Lamb**, as the text for a set of questions.

1. Mary had a little lamb
   Whose fleece was white as snow.
   And everywhere that Mary went,
   The lamb was sure to go.

2. It followed her to school one day
   Which was against the rules.
   It made the children laugh and play
   To ___(4)___ a lamb at school.

Many tests are based on multiple-choice responses. You are given a choice of four (sometimes three) possible answers (options) to choose from.

1. Who owned a little lamb?
   - A   Mary
   - B   some school children
   - C   a teacher at the school
   - D   Mary's parents

> Some will take the form of a question: You may have to circle a letter or shade a box.

The question could have been framed so that you have to complete a sentence.

2. The lamb was owned by
   - A   Mary
   - B   some school children
   - C   a teacher at the school
   - D   Mary's parents

Some questions may have to do with word or phrase meanings.

3. Choose the word that could best replace *laugh* as used in the text.
   - A   shout
   - B   giggle
   - C   cackle
   - D   joke

(Did you notice the different lay out of the options? They were across the page.)

4. Which word would best go in the space labelled (4) in stanza 2?
   - A   chase
   - B   find
   - C   follow
   - D   see

5. Write the numbers 1 to 4 in the boxes to show the correct order in which events occurred in the rhyme. The first one (1) has been done for you.

1	Mary owned a lamb.
	The lamb followed Mary to school.
	Children at the school laughed at Mary's lamb.
	Mary went off to school.

> Sometimes you might have to work out the sequence in which events occurred.

Some questions are called free response questions. You will have to write an answer.

6. What colour was the lamb? Write your answer on the line? _____

...

Sometimes you might have to decide if something is TRUE or FALSE.

7. Tick the box to show if this statement is TRUE or FALSE.
   Lambs were allowed at the school.   TRUE ☐   FALSE ☐

There will be times when you will have to read the whole text and make a judgement.

8. You know that Mary was a kind person because she
   - A   always went to school
   - B   kept the lamb's fleece clean
   - C   let the lamb follow her about
   - D   played in the snow with her pet

9. There might be a question about the use of language in the text.
   The phrase: *white as snow* (line 2), is an example of a
   - A   metaphor
   - B   simile

10. Sometimes you might have to decide if, according to the text, a statement is FACT or OPINION (no example available from the text).
   Answers: 1. A, 2. A, 3. B, 4. D, 5. (1, 3, 4, 2), 6. white, 7. FALSE, 8. C, 9. simile

Understanding Year 5 Comprehension
A. Horsfield © Five Senses Education © W. Marlin

This is a practice page. (The answers follow the questions)

Read the recount *The Tuk-Tuk Ride.*

The Tuk-Tuk Ride

I had my first tuk-tuk ride in Cambodia. The name tuk-tuk is used to describe a motorcycle with a fancy trailer for passengers. Tuk-tuks are the most common form of urban transport in Phnom Peng. Around markets and temple complexes tuk-tuks provide a convenient form of transport for tourists. You can hire a tuk-tuk and driver by the day.

I was with my grandparents and we decided to go to the local morning markets, which were a couple of kilometres from our hotel. It was much too hot and humid to walk.

Out the front of the hotel were a number of tuk-tuk owners waiting to get some business. Grandma wasn't real sure about tuk-tuk travel in a bustling city. They all drive on the wrong side of the road was her comment.

The first thing to do was choose a tuk-tuk. We chose one called Tuk-Tuk Spiderman. Grandpa had to <u>reach an agreement about</u> the fare down town and back. When this was settled we climbed into the carriage. There was ample room for the three of us.

The smiling driver quickly and expertly manipulated his tuk-tuk through streams of tuk-tuks that seemed to be hurrying down, across, along and around the streets. Grandma reckons they are considerate road users. We saw no _____(6)_____ or frustrated drivers.

We arrived outside the markets and the driver helped us out making sure we were safe from the passing traffic.

We expected the driver to leave to find another fare. We were going to be an hour, but he just waited at no extra cost. When we were ready to return he helped us into our carriage and then headed to the hotel.

It was a great way to see the city streets - better than a bus! We were so pleased with the trip Grandpa gave the driver a tip. That got a big smile.

We decided to use Spiderman again when we went for a Cambodian meal that night.

A typical tuk-tuk

Understanding Recounts   Circle a letter or write an answer for questions 1 to 8.

1. What did the family decide to do one morning in Phnom Penh?
    A   go for a Spiderman ride
    B   go to the local markets
    C   go to a place for dinner
    D   go to another hotel

2. What was Grandma's fear about traffic in Cambodia?
    A   the carriages were pulled by a motor cycles
    B   you had to negotiate the fare before the ride
    C   the tuk-tuk couldn't carry enough passengers
    D   tuk-tuk drivers drive on the wrong side of the road

3. What pulls the tuk-tuk carriage?

    Write your answer in the box. [   ]

4. How many people took the tuk-tuk carriage ride to the markets?
    A   1   B   2   C   3   D   4

5. Write the numbers 1 to 4 in the boxes to show the correct order in which events occurred in the recount. The first one (1) has been done for you.

    | | the family decides to visit a market going by tuk-tuk |
    | | the Tuk-Tuk Spiderman waits for the family for the return trip |
    | | the grandfather negotiates a price for a tuk-tuk ride |
    | 1 | the family go to Cambodia for a holiday |

6. A word has been deleted from the text.
    Which word would be best suited to the space (6)?
    A   accidents   B   policemen   C   sights   D   animals

7. Which word means the same as *reach an agreement about price?*
    A   negotiate   B   badger   C   accept   D   suffer

8. Who was most wary about the tuk-tuk trip to the markets?
    A   the narrator
    B   grandma
    C   the tuk-tuk driver
    D   grandpa

Answers: 1. B   2. D   3. a motorbike (cycle)   4. C   5. (2,4,3,1)   6. A   7. A   8. B

Understanding Year 5 Comprehension
A. Horsfield © Five Senses Education © W. Marlin

1. What did the family decide to do one morning in Phnom Penh?
   A   go for a Spiderman ride
   B   go to the local markets
   C   ...ge to a place for dinner
   D   go to another hotel

2. What was Grandma's fear about traffic in Cambodia?
   A   the sam...as were p...lited by a motor cycles
   B   you had to negotiate the fare before the ride
   C   the tuk-tuk couldn't carry enough passengers
   D   tuk-tuk drivers drive on the wrong side of the road

3. What pulls the tuk-tuk carriage?
   Write your answer in the box.

4. How many people took the tuk-tuk carriage ride to the markets?
   A   1   B   2   C   3   D   4

5. Write the numbers 2 to 4 in the boxes to show the correct order in which events occurred in the recount. The first one (1) has been done for you.

   the family decides to visit a market going by tuk-tuk
   the Tuk Tuk driver man waits for the family for the return trip
   the grandfather negotiates a price for a tuk-tuk ride
   the family go to Cambodia for a holiday   1

6. A word has been deleted from the text.
   Which word would be best suited to the space (a)?
   A   accidents   B   pollicebism   C   sights   D   animals

7. Which word means the same as roadim m agreement about rules?
   A   negotiate   B   badget   C   accept   D   suffer

8. Who was most wary about the tuk-tuk trip to the markets?
   A   the narrator
   B   grandma
   C   the tuk-tuk driver
   D   grandpa

Answers: 1 B   2 D   3 a motorbike (cycle)   C   (2 4 3 1)   C   A   A   B

Year 5 Comprehension Passages and Exercises

Each of the 40 passages has a set of eight questions - comprehension and language questions, based upon that text. Following the questions is a section called **Lit Tip** (short for Literacy Tips). These are gems of information that are intended to develop the child's responses to Language Conventions questions arising in texts and tests. They may also be beneficial when answering questions in Language Convention (Grammar) papers or when completing Writing assessment tasks.

Number	Text type	Title	Lit Tip	Page
1	Narrative	Those Poor Plants!	More precise words than said	2 - 3
2	Poetry	The City Dump	Unusual plurals	4 - 5
3	Persuasion	Christmas Lights 1	Phrases	6 - 7
4	Explanation	What is a Hammer?	The suffix ess	8 - 9
5	Report	Curtain Fig	Triple compound words	10 - 11
6	Folk tale	The Tsunami	Similes and clichés	12 - 13
7	Procedure	Sugarcane Milling	Gender	14 - 15
8	Description	Climb on Board	Singular verbs	16 - 17
9	Persuasion	Icecream Van Flyer	The prefix pre	18 - 19
10	Explanation	What are Verbs?	Tense	20 - 21
11	Persuasion	Dogs in Cars	Apostrophes for plurals	22 - 23
12	Poetry	What Will You Be?	Being precise	24 - 25
13	Narrative	The Skateboard	Metaphors	26 - 27
14	Explanation	What is a Quandong?	Collective nouns	28 - 29
15	Report	Precious Gold	Abstract nouns	30 - 31
16	Description	Bat-wing Cannibal Fly	Homophones	32 - 33
17	Explanation	Gone Phishing	Using question marks	34 - 35
18	Report	The Final Kombi	Analogies	36 - 37
19	Poetry	The Microbe	Possessive pronouns	38 - 39
20	Report	Origins of Tea	Being precise	40 - 41
21	Explanation	Redundancies	Singular nouns, final s	42 - 43
22	Persuasion	Christmas Lights 2	Word building	44 - 45
23	Procedure	How to Whistle	Onomatopoeia	46 - 47
24	Review	Tokaanu Thermal Walk	Alliteration	48 - 49
25	Report	Where in Australia?	Comparative adjectives	50 -51
26	Narrative	The Fly Trap	Euphemisms	52 - 53
27	Graphic text	Comic Strips	Writing addresses	54 - 55
28	Play Script	Summer Fun	Non sentences	56 - 57
29	Description	The Humble Spade	The prefix a	58 - 59
30	Persuasion	Letter to Editor	Persuasive text words	60 - 61
31	Explanation	Land Sailing	Brackets	62 - 63
32	Persuasion	Charlotte's Web	Articles: a, an, the	64 - 65
33	Narrative	The Antique Store	Punctuation in speech	66 - 67
34	Procedure	Draw an Eiffel Tower	Slang	68 - 69
35	Report	Water Puppets	Legends, myths, fables	70 - 71
36	Procedure	Have a Safe Summer	Prefixes for numbers	72 - 73
37	Recount	Pro Hart	Interjections	74 - 75
38	Poetry	Bosley	Paired nouns	76 - 77
39	Report	The World's Longest Cliffs	Using indefinite articles	78 - 79
40	Narrative	Yuri's New School	Poor story beginnings	80 - 81

Understanding Year 5 Comprehension
A. Horsfield © Five Senses Education © W. Marlin

Those Poor Plants!

"People poke fun at plants all the time," Dusty finally said, with a sigh.

I felt confused so I shrugged. I wondered if he was joking. Was there a great gap in my education? I was about to find out.

"It's how they talk about them," explained Dusty as if it was obvious. Not to me.

"Take the word 'lemon'," he explained. "People call anything badly made 'a lemon!' Especially cars. How do you think that makes a lemon feel?"

I hadn't really thought about it.

"Then there's 'couch potato'. Do potatoes like to be called lazy? No way!" Bindi chirped in.

"People say things without thinking. Corny, nutty, dill. It just goes on and on," Dusty sounded exasperated.

"Not to mention rhubarb! Rhubarb! Rhubarb! Rhubarb!" Bindi stated angrily.

"Listen for the sniggers when someone says 'leek'!" muttered Dusty, his head lowered.

"Hayseed!" growled Bindi.

"Cauliflower ear!" Dusty's turn.

Bindi: "Raspberry!" Followed by a juicy, rude raspberry splutter.

Dusty: "Sucker!"

Bindi: "Gooseberry."

Dusty: "Sour grapes!"

I was getting a stiff neck glancing from one to the other. It was like watching a tennis match.

'dandelions'

"Wet-the-bed!" snapped Bindi. I hoped she wasn't talking to me.

Dusty came to my rescue. "The name for dandelions, would you believe?" It doesn't make you wet the bed!" he grinned.

"Not all the time!" muttered Bindi. Dusty and I both gave her a surprised glance.

From: The Green Ambulance Caper by A. Horsfield Jojo Publishing 2014

Understanding Narratives   Circle a letter or write an answer for questions 1 to 8.

1. How does Dusty feel about the way plant names are misused?
    He is

    A   amused   B   concerned   C   alarmed   D   miserable

2. Why did Bindi make a rude sound?
    A   she couldn't understand the conversation
    B   she didn't agree with Dusty's comment
    C   she was trying to make her point about raspberries
    D   she tried to explain what a cauliflower ear was

3. If you read the whole story from which the extract was taken, you would expect the story to be

    A   scary   B   informative C   amusing   D   controversial

4. Which line from the text is an example of a simile?

    A   Dusty and I both gave her a surprised glance.

    B   Followed by a juicy, rude raspberry splutter.

    C   Was there a great gap in my education?

    D   It was like watching a tennis match.

5. What does the word *exasperated* mean as used in the text?
    A   doubtfully concerned   B   slightly confused
    C   pleasantly informed   D   highly irritated

6. Which character had the least knowledge of nasty names for plants?
    A   Bindi   B   Dusty   C   the narrator

7. The word *poke* in the first paragraph is
    A   a verb   B   a noun   C   an adjective D   a conjunction

8. What did Dusty and the narrator think Bindi may have done?
    A   wet the bed
    B   picked dandelions
    C   forgotten the explanation
    D   lost interest in the conversation

Need to try another narrative passage? Check the contents page.

Lit Tip 1 – Improve your literacy skills   More precise words than said

It is easy to overuse the word said in story writing. More precise words are available which can improve your story writing.

Look at these three examples:

1. Jack said, "Go away."   2. Jack snapped, "Go away."   3. Jack groaned, "Go away."

Examples 2 and 3 give the reader some insight into Jack's feelings.

Find three better words than said from the text that help you understand how the speaker is feeling.
1. _____   2. _____   3. _____

Understanding Year 5 Comprehension
A. Horsfield © Five Senses Education © W. Marlin

The City Dump

City asleep
City asleep:
Papers fly at the garbage heap.

Refuse dumped and
The seagulls reap
Grapefruit rinds
And coffee grinds
And apple peels.

The seagulls reel and
The field mice steal
In for a bite
At the end of the night
Of crusts and crumbs
And pits of plums.

The white eggshells
And the green-blue smells
And the grey gull's cry
And the red dawn sky . . .

City asleep
City asleep:
A carnival
On the garbage heap.

Felice Holman

Understanding Poetry   Circle a letter or write an answer for questions 1 to 8.

1. When the field mice look for food at the dump they
    A   scurry about excitedly
    B   sneak around quietly
    C   wait patiently until sunrise
    D   find scraps immediately

2. How do the animals at the city dump feel at night?
    A   They are desperate to find food.
    B   They are annoyed by the bad smells.
    C   They are having a great time.
    D   They are tired and ready to sleep.

3. Which word from the poem rhymes with *crumbs*?
    Write your answer in the box.

4. What are the seagulls doing?
    A   flying in circles above the dump   B   looking for eggshells
    C   chasing the field mice   D   avoiding the flying paper

5. The field mice are most likely to leave the dump when
    A   no food scraps are left   B   the seagulls arrive
    C   the city goes to sleep   D   dawn breaks

6. Which word best describes how people in the city react to activity at the dump?
    A   annoyed   B   puzzled   C   unaware   D   interested

7. What would be another name for the pits of plums?
    A   nuts   B   seeds   C   stalks   D   holes

8. The poem, *The City Dump*, makes a contrast between the
    A   seagulls and the paper flying over the dump
    B   food and the smells at the dump
    C   way seagulls and mice scavenge in the dump
    D   sleeping city and the busy dump at night

Need to try another poem? Check the contents page.

Lit Tip 2 - Improve your literacy skills   **Unusual plurals**

To make the plural form of most nouns you simply add an *s*: shoe / shoes
If the noun ends with a consonant + *y*, change the *y* to *i* and add *es*: baby / babies

There are some unusual plural forms. The plural of *mouse* is *mice* (as used in the poem).
Look at these singulars and their plural forms: tooth / teeth, sheep / sheep, man / men
child / children
Can you find the plural form for these nouns? goose _____,wolf _____

salmon _____,woman _____,cactus _____,medium _____

Understanding Year 5 Comprehension
A. Horsfield © Five Senses Education © W. Marlin

Read the persuasive text *Christmas Lights.*

Jannine Wilcox wrote this text about decorating houses with Christmas lights.

Christmas Lights

Our family loves Christmas and the lighting displays put on by individual families or whole streets. They create such a festive feeling in a world that seems to have so many dire problems. There is a feeling of excitement and anticipation amongst the people, especially the children, touring the streets at night to smile and point with glee at the lavish celebrations of the Christmas spirit. The oohs and ahhs seem to capture this feeling of goodwill. It is a pleasure to see happy people in our often dreary streets.

Christmas lights are an example of community spirit. Whole streets are organised to make the world a better place, even if for just a few weeks. Most of the year people are too involved with work, school or financial problems to have time for community involvement.

Christmas lights revive a grand tradition.

It is not true to say the cost of the displays is expensive. People collect bits and pieces for their displays over many years. After Christmas they are taken down and stored for the next festive season for no cost at all. Most lights now-a-days run on very little power, in fact, many have small solar power storing units incorporated into the system. Cheap and safe low voltage power!

The most important point is that ordinary people, including the elderly, have taken over the streets. With all the lights and groups of people the streets are once again safe. Criminals avoid places where their misdeeds are easily seen. Council may still have extravagant displays in the city centres, but local street displays give easy access to local families.

Jannine Wilcox

(Adapted from an unknown source.)

Note: There is another point of view expressed in text No. 22. You might like to compare the opinions given.

Understanding Persuasion

Circle a letter to answer questions 1 to 8.

1. Which option best describes how Jannine feels about Christmas light decorations?
   Jannine feels Christmas lights

   A   frighten young children   B   do not improve dreary streets
   C   are left up for too long   D   create a joyful community

2. According to the writer, families keep their cost of Christmas lighting down by

   A   only using solar powered lights
   B   reusing Christmas lights year after year
   C   sharing lights with others in the street
   D   visiting city displays provided by the council

3. Jannine suggests that for most of the year streets where she lives are

   A   drab   B   unsafe
   C   exciting   D   busy

4. The writer describes the world as having <u>dire</u> problems.
   A *dire* problem is one that is

   A   artificial   B   serious   C   endless   D   sinister

5. Jannine believes that Christmas lights

   A   are too costly   B   create community problems
   C   deter criminals   D   upset young children

6. Which of the following sentences from the text is an opinion?

   A   Our family loves Christmas and the lighting displays.
   B   Most lights now-a-days run on very little power.
   C   Council may still have extravagant displays in the city centres.
   D   The oohs and ahhs seem to capture this feeling of goodwill.

7. Who gets the most pleasure from Christmas street decorations?

   A   the elderly   B   children   C   councils   D   workers

8. How does Jannine feel about decorating houses with Christmas lights?
   Jannine feels it

   A   is a worthwhile activity   B   provides opportunities for criminals
   C   is rather childish   D   wastes time and money

Need to try another persuasion passage? Check the contents page.

Lit Tip 3 – Improve your literacy skills   **Phrases**

Phrases are small groups of words that do not contain a verb.
Some phrases describe nouns or pronouns. They do the work of adjectives. They are called adjectival phrases. Such phrases can make your writing more interesting.
Quite often they begin with a preposition (e.g. in, near, under, with, of).

Examples of phrases: The girl <u>with the red hair</u> is late. The car <u>in the shed</u> was old.
Underline the phrases in these sentences

1. The house on the hill belongs to the mayor.   2. I saw a frog under the bush.
3. The tree by the fence has died.   4. Meg's shoes near the step are wet.

Understanding Year 5 Comprehension
A. Horsfield © Five Senses Education © W. Marlin

What is a Hammer?

Many households have a small hammer in a convenient location in the home for minor maintenance work. Hammers come in a wide variety of weights and sizes.

A hammer is a simple tool designed to manually drive in nails, pins, tacks, and other fasteners into softer materials, such as wood or drywall. A hammer has a head and a handle, or shaft. The type of head depends on how the hammer is to be used, but most have a face that strikes the fastener behind the bell and neck, which holds the handle. The opposite ends of the head may have a forked nail-puller (as in a claw hammer) and a peen* (small face for driving pins or tacks). Most builders' and household hammers are claw hammers.

How to Safely Use a Hammer

To safely use a claw hammer, select the weight appropriate to the nail size (or tack) to be struck. Lightly hold the fastener in position with one hand. Firmly grasp the lower half of the handle then slowly swing the flat head face to tap the nail head firmly and squarely. This will secure the nail in position. Make sure your fingers cannot be struck by the hammerhead. Then swing the hammer with more force to drive the head into the wood. It may take a couple of hits.

How to Maintain a Hammer

Hammers require no maintenance. The head of a wood-handled hammer can be replaced when the metal deteriorates. Replacement handles and installation wedges are available at hardware stores. The metal wedge is driven into the head end of the handle to hold the head tightly on the handle.

Some types of hammers

| **Club hammer** | **Cross and straight peen hammer** | **Ball peen hammer** | **Claw hammer** |
| for demolition jobs | for metal work | for shaping metal | for woodworking |

* Peen refers to the end of a hammer head opposite the flat face, often V-shaped or curved.
Adapted from: http://home.howstuffworks.com/hammer.htm

Understanding Explanations   Circle a letter or write an answer for questions 1 to 8.

1. Which of these hammers is most likely to be the heaviest?

   A   club hammer
   B   cross and straight peen hammer
   C   ball peen hammer
   D   claw hammer

2. A claw hammer can best be used for

   A   shaping metal
   B   breaking up bricks
   C   driving or removing nails
   D   repairing motor vehicles

3. What is required when a handle has to be replaced?

   A   fasteners
   B   a metal wedge
   C   a claw
   D   a peen

4. Which type of hammer is a carpenter most likely to use?

   A   club hammer
   B   cross and straight peen hammer
   C   ball peen hammer
   D   claw hammer

5. Which of the following is a fastener **NOT** for use with a small claw hammer?

   A   nail   B   tack   C   screw   D   panel pin

6. What warning is given when hammering a nail into timber?

   A   be careful not to break the hammer handle
   B   take care not to hit your fingers
   C   do not damage the timber near the nail
   D   choose a ball peen hammer of the right weight

7. Which hammer would be most useful for smashing up old chairs?

   Write your answer on the line. _____

8. What does the word *peen* refer to in a claw hammer?

   A   the flat metal face for driving fasteners
   B   the metal wedge used to secure the handle to the head
   C   the wooden shaft of the hammer
   D   the ball shape end of metal-working hammers

Need to try another explanation passage? Check the contents page.

Lit Tip 4 - Improve your literacy skills   **The suffix *ess***

The suffix *ess* is often used to distinguish a male from a female.
Examples: A lion<u>ess</u> is a female lion. A princ<u>ess</u> is a royal female.
A godd<u>ess</u> is a female god.
A female that teaches children in a private home is a govern<u>ess</u>.

Can you find the female term for: tiger _____, emperor _____

The wife of a duke is a _____.   The wife of a count is a _____.

Note: It is now considered unacceptable to distinguish between most male and female jobs using the *ess* suffix for females. We don't say actress. People on the stage are all actors. We no longer use the terms waitress, hostess or stewardess.

Understanding Year 5 Comprehension
A. Horsfield © Five Senses Education © W. Marlin

The Curtain Fig

Near Yungaburra (north Queensland), is the famous Curtain Fig (*Ficus virens*). The tree stands 50m tall and spreads to 39m wide at the base. It is at least 800 years old.

The curtain effect has resulted from the weight of the fig tree being so great that the host tree fell over landing on a 45° angle. The strangler fig has grown along the slanting angle of the leaning tree dangling 15m to the ground, thereby forming a curtain. An information board describes the process.

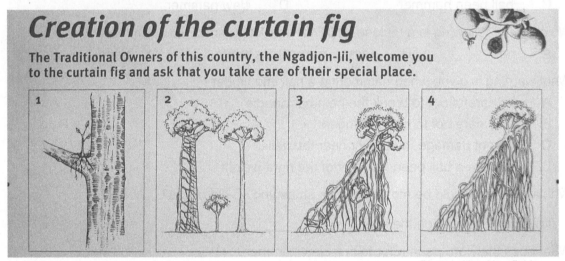

Creation of the curtain fig
The Traditional Owners of this country, the Ngadjon-Jii, welcome you to the curtain fig and ask that you take care of their special place.

Photo : Alan Horsfield

From the information board.

1. A seed was deposited in bird droppings in the host tree's crown. It germinated and the first roots descended to the soil.

2. Enriched by the soil, the fig developed aerial roots, which encircled the tree and eventually strangled the host tree.

3. The host tree then fell into a neighbouring tree - a stage unique to the curtain fig tree. Vertical fig roots descended from the fig's trunk to form a curtain-like appearance.

4. Eventually the host tree rotted away leaving a free standing fig tree.

Normally these fig seeds germinate in a tree and try to grow roots into the ground.

Once this important step is achieved, the fig will grow vigorously, finally strangling the hosting tree and then grow on independently. In this case, the hosting tree tilted towards the next one. The fig also grew around that tree. Its curtain of aerial roots drops 15m to the ground.

Understanding Reports   Circle a letter or write an answer for questions 1 to 8.

1. In years, how old is the Curtain Fig estimated to be?

    A   39   B   45   C   50   D   800

2. What is the reason the words (*Ficus virens*) are written in brackets and in italics?

    A   to make the reader aware that they are not English words

    B   it makes the report look more interesting

    C   they are provided for people who want to check the facts in the report

    D   it provides the reader with the tree's scientific name

3. Where did the Curtain Fig seed germinate?

    A   on the branch of a host tree   B   in the soil under a host tree

    C   between two trees   D   on a fallen dead tree

4. The Curtain Fig's source of food comes from

    A   rotting wood   B   the sap of another tree

    C   the soil   D   nutrients in the air

5. The Curtain Fig's first roots developed in

    A   moist soil   B   the air

    C   water   D   the bark of a tree

6. A plant that is a parasite

    A   does not need moisture to survive   B   has roots that reach for the ground

    C   lives off another tree's sap   D   lives under another tree

7. Do all strangler figs form a curtain?

    Tick a box.   YES ☐   NO ☐

8. The Curtain Fig killed its host tree by

    A   draining sap from the host tree

    B   choking the host tree with its roots

    C   taking nutrients from the soil near the host tree

    D   pulling the host tree to the ground

Need to try another report? Check the contents page.

Understanding Year 5 Comprehension
A. Horsfield © Five Senses Education © W. Marlin

A Japanese Folk Tale

The earthquake and tsunami disasters that have hit Japan have been devastating. They presented the people with incredible pain and suffering, and the death of loved ones. These events have people reaching out to support one another in <u>tragic</u> times.

Tsunamis are often portrayed in Asian art works.

This is a traditional Japanese story but the story could be from many places in Asia.

Kino lives in Japan. His son worries about the disasters that hit Japan.

"We must learn to live with danger," said Kino's father.

"Do you mean the ocean and the volcano cannot hurt us if we're not afraid?" asked Kino.

"No I did not mean that. The ocean is there. The volcano is there. It is true any day a storm may whip up the seas and the water will rise. A volcano may burst into fire and smoke. We must accept this fate, but without fear. We must tell ourselves that someday we must die and it does not matter if it's because of the ocean or because of the volcano, or whether we grow old and weak."

"I don't want to think about such things," said Kino.

"It is right for you not to think about them," said his father. "Then do not be afraid. When you are afraid you are thinking about them all the time. Enjoy life and do not fear death – that is the way of a very good Japanese."

Adapted from:
http://www.storytimeyoga.com/blog/japanese-tsunami-folk-tale-to-tell-in-this-time-of-tragedy/#sthash.ATULHGID.dpuf

Understanding Folk Tales Circle a letter to answer questions 1 to 8.

1. Which is Kino's father's opinion?
   - A   volcanic eruptions are worse than tsunamis
   - B   people should avoid danger
   - C   everyone will die of some cause
   - D   sons should ask their fathers for advice

2. Kino's father suggests that being fearful and worryng?
   - A   prevents people from being killed in disasters
   - B   causes people to grow old and weak
   - C   stops people from enjoying life
   - D   helps people to prepare for disasters

3. The words of Kino's father to his son could best be described as
   - A   advice   B   a warning   C   a threat   D   praise

4. The word tragic is used in the text. A word with a similar meaning would be
   - A   gruesome   B   disastrous   C   unexpected   D   unhappy

5. A traditional story is one that
   - A   has been passed down through generations
   - B   is used to explain unusual natural events
   - C   has to do with life and death
   - D   was once true but is no longer important

6. In Japan, earthquakes and tsunamis result in people
   - A   blaming others for their misfortunes
   - B   becoming involved in disputes
   - C   providing care for one another
   - D   telling their children folk tales

7. What does Kino's father say causes the sea to rise?
   - A   big storms   B   tsunamis   C   earthquakes D   eruptions

8. Kino's father says people must
   - A   keep clear of volcanoes   B   look for safe places to live
   - C   be afraid of disasters   D   accept whatever happens

---

Lit Tip 6 - Improve your literacy skills   Similes and Clichés
A simile is a figure of speech comparing one thing with another. It can help to make your writing clearer and more interesting and emphasise a point.
Examples: His skin was as rough **as** the bark of a tree.
          The speedboat skimmed the water **like** a swallow.
Similes often use the words *as* and *like*.
Similes that are overused are called clichés. They do not improve your writing.
Examples: Jack was as white as a ghost. The wind was as cold as ice.

Complete this with a simile (no clichés): The cat's fur was as _____ .

Understanding Year 5 Comprehension
A. Horsfield © Five Senses Education © W. Marlin

Sugar Cane Milling

Australian farmers grow sugar cane to extract sugar. However, sugarcane can be used for numerous other products.

'Raw' sugar is the main product of Australian sugar cane. There are a host of other uses for the plant. Every single part of the sugar cane plant is used.

At the sugar mill sugar is taken out of the stalk through a crushing process. The left-over fibre from the stalk is called bagasse. It is the dry dusty pulp that remains after juice is extracted from sugar cane.

Bagasse is used to power the sugar cane mill. The mill can make its own electricity by burning the bagasse, which means it doesn't have to rely on fossil fuels (e.g. coal) to power the mill. Sugarcane is the only crop in the world that can do this.

This flow chart shows the process for making sugar from cane.

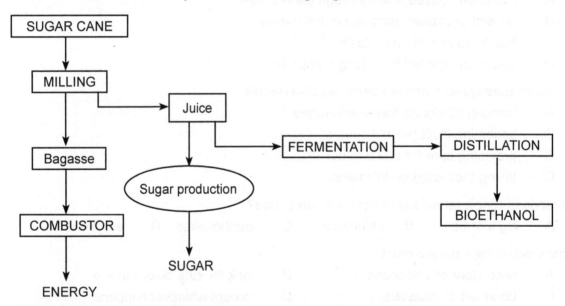

Other by-products include residue which can be used as fertilizer on cane farms and gardens. The by-products are also used in the making of plastics, clothing and medicines.

Molasses is a dark syrup separated from the raw sugar crystals during the milling process.

It is used as a raw material for ethanol (as a petrol additive for cars) - and rum. It can also be used for animal feed.

Sugar cane is a truly versatile agricultural product.
Adapted from: The journey of a jelly bean produced by CANEGROWERS.

Understanding Procedures

Circle a letter, write an answer or tick a box for questions 1 to 8.

1. The flow chart is a diagram used to show
   - A   the importance of sugar cane mills
   - B   what workers do in a sugar mill
   - C   how sugar cane is processed
   - D   the fastest way to get sugar from sugar cane

2. What is bagasse?
   - A   a natural gas used to heat boilers
   - B   the dried fibre of crushed sugar cane
   - C   the juice crushed from sugar cane stalks
   - D   a waste product from the milling of cane

3. The word *agricultural* has a similar meaning to
   - A   farming   B   useful   C   plentiful   D   cooking

4. In the flow chart there is a label for COMBUSTOR.
   A combustor is
   - A   the combination of bagasse and sugar cane juice
   - B   the first crushing of sugar cane from cane fields
   - C   a name for bagasse when it is used as fuel
   - D   a place where energy is produced to run machinery

5. Look at the flow chart. What product is sugar obtained from?

   Write your answer on the line. _____

6. After the sugar cane juice has fermented it
   - A   is used as ethanol in fuel for cars   B   becomes energy for use in combustors
   - C   goes through a distillation process   D   is turned in to fertiliser for farmers

7. What is the last product extracted from the sugar cane?
   - A   juice   B   bioethanol   C   bagasse   D   molasses

8. What product from the sugar milling can be used as stock feed?
   - A   raw sugar   B   residue   C   bagasse   D   molasses

Need to try another procedure? Check the contents page.

Lit Tip 7 - Improve your literacy skills   **What is gender?**
Gender applies to nouns and pronouns. There are four categories of gender.

Masculine: **Nouns** - man, king, bull.   **Pronouns** - he, his.
Feminine: **Nouns** - woman, queen, cow.   **Pronouns** - her, she.
Neuter: (Neither male nor female) **Nouns** - road, fence. **Pronoun** - it.
Common: (Either male or female) **Nouns** - child, cattle. **Pronoun** - them.

Using initials (M, F, N, C) write the gender of the underlined words on the line beneath.
The king along with his stately wife waved to the crowd along the street.

____   ____   ____   ____   ____

Understanding Year 5 Comprehension
A. Horsfield © Five Senses Education © W. Marlin

Climb on Board

Mikki glanced around. No one was watching.

Still she hesitated. There could be someone she hadn't seen on one of the other fishing boats in the marina.

It was time to make a decision. She leapt over the small gap between the harbour wall and the stern of the sleek fishing boat, Gotcha. She had a moment's difficulty before regaining her balance as the boat rode on the lapping water. She was a landlubber not a sailor. Good old dry land was her natural habitat.

She ducked through the cabin door and found herself in a small public area. It was not as luxurious as she expected. She stood still for a few seconds listening for any strange sounds.

Looking around she realised the space was basically the kitchen or galley area. Brown padded bench seats tightly abutted the legs of a worn vinyl-topped table. Behind it was a high seat in front of the wheel and the control panel.

Five paces to the right took Mikki to the narrow steps down and into a bedroom in the bow. The cabin had a small shower, a hand basin and a toilet. Mikki stood still. She could hear the sea lapping against the sides of the boat. She could feel the gentle rocking. She didn't like it. She needed to sit down. She sat on the narrow bed.

She became aware of the smell of stale cigarette smoke. It smelt like the TV room in her grandfather's place. She pulled a monkey face. Her queasiness was getting worse. She sucked on her lips and was about to dizzily stand up when she heard footsteps on the deck above.

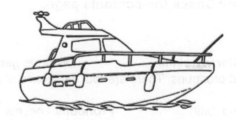

Understanding Descriptions Circle a letter or write an answer for questions 1 to 8.

1. What concerned Mikki the most?
    - A   the rocking of the boat would make her seasick
    - B   falling into the water when jumping aboard
    - C   she would get caught for being on the boat
    - D   the unpleasant smell in the small bedroom

2. Mikki feels she is a *landlubber*, not a sailor. A *landlubber* is a person who
    - A   is unfamiliar with the sea
    - B   loves to go fishing
    - C   prefers to be a passenger
    - D   takes unnecessary risks

3. This description is most likely part of a
    - A   explanation   B   warning   C   report   D   narrative

4. Mikki didn't like the rocking motion of the boat. She also did **not** like the
    - A   sound of lapping water
    - B   smell of stale smoke
    - C   worn vinyl-topped table
    - D   brown padded bench seats

5. Write the numbers 1 to 4 in the boxes to show the correct order in which events occurred in the text. The first one (1) has been done for you.

	Mikki enters the galley
	Mikki hears footsteps
1	Mikki jumps onto the boat
	Mikki feels queasy

6. When Mikki heard footsteps she was
    - A   on the harbour wall
    - B   hiding in the galley
    - C   sitting on a bed
    - D   near the boat's control panel

7. The boat Mikki jumps onto is called *Gotcha*. *Gotcha* most likely refers to catching
    - A   intruders   B   fish   C   landlubbers   D   sailors

8. What would be a suitable alternate title for the passage?
    - A   The Intruder   B   The Marina   C   Footsteps Above   D   A Strange Cabin

Need to try another description? Check the contents page.

Lit Tip 8 – Improve your literacy skills   Singular verbs

We usually think of words that end with s as being a plural form of nouns.
We often add an s to verbs. This makes them **singular** verbs!
Examples: walks, flips, corrects, drives, sells.

In sentences, singular nouns must be used with singular verbs.
Example: The <u>nurse</u> <u>makes</u> the bed.
Nurse is a singular noun and *makes* is a singular verb. In grammar we say the noun and verb must agree.

Add a suitable singular verb to complete these sentences.
1. Jack _____ cricket after school.   2. The plant _____ in a pot.

3. A sprinter _____ very quickly.   4. My wrist _____ when I write.

Understanding Year 5 Comprehension
A. Horsfield © Five Senses Education © W. Marlin

Read the flyer for the *Ice Cream Van.*

Gerry found this flyer in his family's letterbox during the summer school holidays.

Holiday's Ice Cream

This summer let the
ice cream man come to you!

You can call us and we deliver or you can catch us when
you hear our catchy, merry tune come into your street.

If you miss out you can catch us at the south end of Four Mile Beach.
Look for my brightly painted van.

We have a host of traditional flavours including our original <u>bush tucker</u>
flavours of wattle seed, quondong and native bee honey.

Your choice of cones, wafers,
on sticks or between biscuits

We also supply for parties and social events.

Order on-line for quick service.

Understanding Persuasions Circle a letter to answer questions 1 to 8.

1. Where did Gerry find the ice cream flier?

    A   on the ice cream van   B   in a holiday park

    C   in the family letter box   D   at an ice cream shop

2. The owner of the ice cream van attracts the attention of customers by

    A   parking on Four Mile Beach   B   playing a catchy tune

    C   having many different flavours D   advertising on his van

3. Holiday's ice cream has *bush tucker* flavours. *Bush tucker* is food

    A   from edible native Australian plants

    B   that hasn't been processed in a factory

    C   of lower quality than farm produce

    D   that is an alternative to processed food

4. An ice cream buyer **cannot** get an ice cream from the ice cream van

    A   on a stick   B   in a cone

    C   between two biscuits   D   in a cup or tub

5. When does the ice cream van operate?

    A   on weekends   B   after school

    C   during the summer   D   Mondays to Fridays

6. For quick service Holiday's ice cream van recommends that buyers should

    A   choose ice creams in cones   B   place orders on-line

    C   have a party   D   listen for his catchy tune

7. Which word from the text is a compound word?

    A   biscuits   B   quondong   C   deliver   D   letterbox

8. What would be a big benefit of getting ice creams from Holiday's ice cream van?

    A   ice creams are delivered to the home

    B   music is played when ice creams are bought

    C   there are many traditional flavoured ice creams

    D   the van is parked at the south end of Four Mile Beach

Need to try another persuasion passage? Check the contents page.

Lit Tip 9 - Improve your literacy skills   The prefix *pre*

Prefixes - groups of letters attached to the front of words to change their meaning.
Pre before words changes the meaning to mean *before* or *previous* to.
Examples: pre<u>dict</u> - estimate when things will happen before they do
          pre<u>vent</u> - stop something happening before it could happen
Draw a line to match the pre word with its meaning.
A preschool   1. to see something (a film) before it's released to the public
B preview   2. to do something before food deteriorates
C preserve   3. the first in importance
D premier   4. education before school starts

And *prefix*: letters placed before the base meaning of a word.
          Now *prepare* for the next page of exercises!

Understanding Year 5 Comprehension
A. Horsfield © Five Senses Education © W. Marlin

What are Verbs?

A verb is a part of speech. Other parts of speech include nouns and adjectives. Verbs are doing words. They can express:

• a physical action (e.g. to run, to ride, to climb)

• a mental action (e.g. to think, to guess, to consider)

• a state of being (e.g. to be, to exist, to appear)

Verbs which express a state of being are the most difficult to spot, but they are the most common. The most common verb is the verb to be. That's the one which goes:

Subject (using pronouns)	Verb **to be** in the past tense	Verb **to be** in the present tense	Verb **to be** in the future tense
I	was	am	will be
You	were	are	will be
He / She / It	was	is	will be
We	were	are	will be
You	were	are	will be
They	were	are	will be

We mostly use these verbs without thinking about them.

It is the past tense of action and thinking verbs that can become confusing.

For the past tense of most English verbs simply add *ed*. These are called regular verbs. Examples: walk/walked, clap/clapped.

Look at some irregular verbs. These have quite big changes.

We say kept instead of keeped, or bought instead of buyed.

Some common irregular verbs include: bite/bit, blow/blew, eat/ate, write/wrote

There are some verbs that don't change: shut, hurt

Understanding Explanations   Circle a letter or write an answer for questions 1 to 8.

1. Choose the verb that is an action verb.

    A   were   B   believe   C   wonder   D   chase

2. Look at this sentence.   Jack went to the shop after school.
    What tense is the verb *went*?

    A   past tense   B   present tense   C   future tense

3. Chose the correct word to complete this sentence.
    Charles _____ his name in the wet cement!

    A   writ   B   wrote   C   written   D   write

4. What is the past tense of *eat*?
    Write your answer on the line. _____

5. Chose the correct word or words to complete this sentence.
    Linda _____ completed her test paper.

    A   is   B   were   C   has   D   are

6. Choose the verb from these words.

    A   carnival   B   fastest   C   funniest   D   compare

7. According to the text, which statement is CORRECT?

    A   To make the past tense of many verbs simply add *ed* to the verb.

    B   The word *write* is the same for both present tense and past tense.

    C   The past tense of irregular verbs often end in *ed*.

    D   All verbs involve an action.

8. Which of these verbs does the writer feel is most difficult to recognise?

    A   irregular verbs   B   past tense verbs
    C   verbs to be   D   future tense of verbs

Need to try another explanation? Check the contents page.

Lit Tip 10 - Improve your literacy skills   **What is tense?**

Did you have a problem with question 2? It asked about *tense*.
The *tense* of verbs tells you when the action happens. There are three main tenses.
Things to know about tense: **Present** tense uses the original form of the verb
                              Past tense verbs have a few patterns
                              Future tense verbs need *will* (shall) + the verb

Look at the regular verb *clean*: I clean my shoes every day. (present tense)
                                   I cleaned my shoes last night. (past tense)
                                   I <u>will clean</u> my shoes tomorrow. (future tense)
Look at the irregular verb *write*: I write my name on the page. (present tense)
                                     I <u>wrote</u> my name on the page. (past tense)
                                     I <u>will write</u> my write my name on the page. (future tense)

What tense are these sentences in? I run a marathon twice a year. _____ tense
                                   I ran a marathon last year. _____ tense
                                   I will run a marathon next year. _____ tense
What is the past tense for think? _____

Understanding Year 5 Comprehension
A. Horsfield © Five Senses Education © W. Marlin

11 Read the persuasive text *Dogs in cars.*

Dogs in Cars

Should dogs be allowed to ride in cars? There is no easy yes or no answer.

For some drivers, it is great to have a companion with them. However, this comfort comes with costs. The biggest problem with dogs in a car is that they are a distraction. Distractions are one of the biggest causes of road accidents.

Firstly, many dogs are unable to stay still for any length of time even in a restrainer. This is a worry. If a dog is moving about in a car it is very hard for a driver not to investigate why the dog is restless. Restless dogs can distract the driver but also they could block the driver's clear vision, making it difficult to judge safe driving especially when lane-changing or coming to an intersection.

It's worse if the dog tries to climb onto the driver's lap or onto the floor under the driver's legs when the car is _____(7)_____!

Some dog owners are convinced that their dogs are well behaved no matter what. Is this always true? Can allowances be made for a few people who believe their dog is better behaved than most? There is no way of testing which dogs are well behaved passengers and safe to drive with.

I realise some dog owners are fond of their pets. They want companionship. If you want a companion, bring a friend who understands the dangers of driver distraction.

Finally, the truth is, most dogs are likely to distract the driver and cause an accident.

Driving can be a dangerous activity. There is no need to introduce more driver distractions.

Adapted from: http://www.helium.com/debates/280127-should-dogs-be-allowed-to-ride-in-cars/side_by_side (02 October 2009)

Understanding Persuasions

Circle a letter to answer questions 1 to 8.

1. What does the writer consider to be the main cause of accidents?
   - A   driver distraction
   - B   dogs under the legs of the driver
   - C   driver comfort
   - D   lane changing without looking

2. What is the reason some drivers might take their dog with them in their car?
   - A   dogs enjoy rides in cars
   - B   dogs get restless if left at home
   - C   dogs are companionship for the driver
   - D   dogs provide protection for the driver

3. The tone of the text suggests the writer
   - A   abhors dogs in cars
   - B   is confused why drivers need dogs in cars
   - C   has never had a dog in a car
   - D   understands why people have dogs in cars

4. The problem with most dogs in cars is that they
   - A   bark too much
   - B   are unable to keep still
   - C   sleep on the back seat
   - D   are ignored by their owners

5. What do some dog owners believe to be true about dogs?
   - A   their own dog is always well behaved in a car
   - B   dogs are better companions than people
   - C   dogs should be tested for good behaviour
   - D   driving with a dog is safe if the dog is restrained

6. The word that best describes how the writer feels about dogs in cars is:
   - A   indifferent
   - B   concerned
   - C   amused
   - D   unfeeling

7. A word has been deleted from the text.
   Which word would be best suited for the space (7)?
   - A   stable
   - B   quiet
   - C   moving
   - D   crowded

8. The text begins with a question. The writer asks this question because he/she
   - A   doesn't have an answer
   - B   is testing the reader's knowledge
   - C   is confused by the topic
   - D   wants to attract the reader's attention

Need to try another persuasion passage? Check the contents page.

Lit Tip 11 – Improve your literacy skills   Possessive form of plural nouns
To make the possessive form of most singular nouns you simply add apostrophe s ('s).

For plural nouns you generally add s + the apostrophe (s').
Examples: boys' noses. The noses belong to a number of boys.

Some nouns change form when they become plurals, e.g. bus/buses, baby/babies
For most similar type words you still add s + the apostrophe (s'): babies' prams
Some nouns have a different word for the plural form, e.g. foot/feet, goose/geese
For such nouns you add apostrophe s ('s), e.g. men's hats, children's playground

Choose the correct punctuation for these. (Cross out the incorrect word.)
(mice's/mices') tails,   (girl's/girls') teams,   women's/womens' party

Understanding Year 5 Comprehension
A. Horsfield © Five Senses Education © W. Marlin

What Will You Be?

They never stop asking me,

"What will you be?

A doctor, a dancer,

A diver at sea?"

They never stop bugging me:

"What will you be?"

As if they expect me to

Stop being me.

When I grow up I'm going to be a Sneeze,

And sprinkle Germs on all my Enemies.

When I grow up I'm going to be a Toad,

And dump all Silly Questions in the road.

When I grow up, I'm going to be a Child.

I'll Play the whole darn day and drive them___(7)___.

Dennis Lee (1939 -   )

Understanding Poetry   Circle a letter or write an answer for questions 1 to 8

1. What emotion does the narrator of the poem feel when questioned?

   A   irritation   B   surprise   C   pride   D   worry

2. Who are most likely the enemies the narrator refers to?

   A   doctors, dancers and divers   B   any other children
   C   pesky adults   D   germs, bugs and toads

3. When the narrator of the poem says, I am going to be a Sneeze, he is being

   A   thoughtless   B   serious   C   civil   D   cheeky

4. Instead of answering silly questions the narrator would prefer to

   A   catch a cold   B   continue being a child
   C   put toads on the road   D   bug the adults

5. *Alliteration* is a technique writers often use.
   Which extract from the text is an example of alliteration?

   A   I'm going to be a Sneeze
   B   sprinkle Germs on all my enemies
   C   a doctor, a dancer / a diver
   D   When I grow up, I'm going to be a Child

   > Alliteration: the use of the same first letter or sound in words close to one another.

6. The narrator suggests he could be three different things when he grows up.
   His suggestions could best be described as

   A   impossible   B   practical   C   reasonable   D   original

7. The last word of the poem has been omitted.
   Chose the most suitable word for the space (7).

   A   mild   B   silly   C   wild   D   insane

8. Which word from the poem rhymes with road?

   Write your answer on the line. _____

Need to try another poem? Check the contents page.

Lit Tip 12 – Improve your literacy skills   Being precise

Using more precise words makes your writing more interesting and enjoyable.

Take the word 'look'. It's a fairly dull word.
Compare the differences in these sentences. 1. Dad examined the diagram.
2. Dad admired the diagram.   3. Dad studied the diagram.
Each one tells the reader something different about Dad.
Collect up a bank of 'look' words you can use. A thesaurus is a great writing tool!

Complete these sentences with better 'look' words to show Mum's feelings.

1.Mum _____ at the mess.   2. Mum _____ at the mess.

Understanding Year 5 Comprehension
A. Horsfield © Five Senses Education © W. Marlin

The Skateboard

'Look at that!' exclaimed Mum peering through the kitchen window.

Dad and I rushed to the window. 'Good grief,' said Dad as I tried to push in for a better look.

'Don't believe it!' added Mum.

I still couldn't see whatever it was that she didn't believe. I pushed my head in front of Dad's elbow and peered out. Then I saw it.

Justine, my older sister, was strutting down the drive with a flashy looking surfboard under her arm. The afternoon sun glinted off its glossy blue and white finish.

'Wow!' I whispered loudly.

We jostled into the garage as Justine gently placed her new board against the wall.

'Looks great,' declared Dad. I think he wished he were twenty years younger. Justine beamed.

'Where did you get the money?' I questioned. I was a little bit envious.

'Been saving for ages. From my work,' explained Justine with a sparkle of pride. Dad and Mum nodded their joint approval.

Justine went on, 'Then a special came up at Ridin' the Waves, near where I work – so I grabbed it.'

I felt peeved but couldn't explain why so I wandered down to the shops with my skateboard like a tired, old man.

No one was there so I sat down on a milk crate behind a small supermarket. Idly I glanced at my old skateboard and thought about Justine's new surfboard.

Distractedly I stood up and skated back to the front of the shops. I stopped in front of the Community Noticeboard. It was covered in tattered ads for all sort of strange things - and a second-hand Speed Devil Aurora skateboard – at half price. It was a rocket on wheels! _____(8)_____ !

Understanding Narratives   Circle a letter or write an answer for questions 1 to 8.

1. What is the most likely reason the narrator felt peeved?
   - A   his parents were being very involved with his sister
   - B   he had to walk to the shops
   - C   he was a little jealous of Justine's purchase
   - D   he didn't have the money for a surfboard

2. Justine got her surfboard from *Ridin' the Waves*. Ridin' the Waves is most likely a
   - A   life saving club house
   - B   fashion outlet
   - C   travel agent
   - D   surf shop

3. Justine placed her board gently against the wall because she
   - A   didn't want to mark the wall
   - B   was being careful with her new board
   - C   knew her parents were watching
   - D   wasn't allowed to make a noise

4. Which of the following from the text is an example of a metaphor?
   - A   covered in tattered ads
   - B   strutting down the drive
   - C   like a tired, old man
   - D   It was a rocket on wheels!

5. What is the most likely reason the narrator whispered when he saw the surfboard?
   - A   he was disappointed
   - B   he was being mean
   - C   he was impressed
   - D   he was depressed

6. The author uses a variety of words instead of *said* to make the text interesting.
   List three words used instead of said.   Answers given are examples only.

   1 _____   2 _____   3 _____

7. What part of speech is *distractedly*?
   - A   adverb   B   noun   C   adjective   D   pronoun

8. A sentence has been deleted from the text.
   What could be an appropriate concluding final sentence (8)?
   - A   I had to have it!
   - B   Justine might buy it for me.
   - C   It had never been used!
   - D   It must be a fake.

Lit Tip 13 – Improve your literacy skills   Metaphors

Did you have a problem with question 4?   What is a metaphor?
A metaphor is a description that says one thing is the same as another thing.
(**Note:** A simile says something is like another thing – check Lit Tip 6.)

Examples: Snow is a white blanket. We all know that snow is not really a blanket!
My bedroom was my prison. A bedroom is not really a prison but to the writer it feels
like a prison.
Tick the boxes for the metaphors in these.

1. The clouds are cotton balls in the sky. ☐   2. Jack is as fast as lightning. ☐

3. Stars are sparkling diamonds. ☐   4. Dad is a couch potato! ☐

Understanding Year 5 Comprehension
A. Horsfield © Five Senses Education © W. Marlin

14 Read the explanation *What is a Quandong?*

What is a Quandong?

The quandong is a unique Australian fruit found in the arid regions of all mainland states.

Ideally adapted to arid environments, the quondong is a semi-parasitic plant. It can survive in soils with high salt levels. They attach themselves to the root system of other trees, shrubs and grasses to supplement their need for nutrients and water. Quandongs are usually found growing in the base of another tree - on the root systems of host plants.

Quandongs have a rough bark and grow to three metres in height, with a dense two metre wide crown of leathery long, hanging leaves.

The cream flowers are small and cup shaped, and hang in clusters at the ends of the outer branches. The flowers form in late summer and the fruit is ready to eat in spring. The shiny, bright scarlet fruit is about the size of a cherry and contains a large kernel, which is sometimes only a little smaller than the fruit.

Traditionally, quandongs have been an important traditional aboriginal fruit. They are tart but highly nutritious and contains twice the vitamin C of an orange. Amongst members of central Australia's Pitjantjara people, quandongs were considered a substitute for meat - especially when hunting game was in short supply. The kernel is also very nutritious. Indigenous Australians often used it for medicinal purposes.

The wood from the slow growing trees was prized for the making of traditional bowls - or coolamons. The quandong fruit feature in aboriginal mythology across all the desert regions of Australia.

The only Australian food plant to be successfully farmed is the Macadamia nut. Will the quandong be our second farmed food plant?

Adapted from: http://www.nullarbornet.com.au/themes/quandongs.html
http://www.outbackpride.com.au/species/quandong

Understanding Explanations

Circle a letter to answer questions 1 to 8.

1. Quandongs get much of their nutrition from
   - A   soils that are mostly dry
   - B   the root systems of host plants
   - C   the dead wood of desert trees
   - D   high salt levels in the soil

2. What is a coolamon?
   - A   a traditional wooden bowl
   - B   a semi-parasitic plant
   - C   the roots system of a plant
   - D   the seed of the quandong

3. The fruit of a quandong looks very similar to
   - A   an apple
   - B   a pear
   - C   a strawberry
   - D   a cherry

4. The quandong fruit is ready to eat in
   - A   autumn
   - B   winter
   - C   summer
   - D   spring

5. According to the text which statement about the quandong kernel is CORRECT?
   - A   the kernel is shiny and bright scarlet
   - B   the kernel has no nutritional value
   - C   the kernel is used by indigenous Australians as a medicine
   - D   the kernel is a little larger than the quandong fruit

6. Which word best describes the taste of a quandong?
   - A   bitter
   - B   sweet
   - C   bland
   - D   salty

7. The quandong is called a *semi-parasitic* plant.
   The prefix semi in this context means
   - A   hardy
   - B   very large
   - C   partly
   - D   second last

8. The writer of the text feels that the quandong
   - A   is a suitable substitute for the Macadamia nut
   - B   could become as popular as the Macadamia nut
   - C   is an alternative to meat in a personal diet
   - D   has no future as a commercial food crop

Need to try another explanation? Check the contents page.

Lit Tip 14 – Improve your literacy skills   Collective nouns

A collective noun is a count noun that stands for a group of individuals, animals or things.
Collective nouns are more precise and interesting than such words as *bunch* or *lots of*.
Some common collective nouns are: **class** of girls, **flock** of sheep, **swarm** of bees.
Although a collective noun represents many, it is a singular noun.
The album of photographs is on the table. (Singular noun, album - singular verb, is).
Incorrect: The album of photographs are on the table.

Choose the verb to complete this sentence: That gang of thugs (rob / robs) banks.

Some collective nouns: herd of cows, library of books, fleet of ships, galaxy of stars
Of course, it is quite acceptable to have a bunch of roses or a bunch of bananas!

Understanding Year 5 Comprehension
A. Horsfield © Five Senses Education © W. Marlin

Precious Gold

Gold was the first metal widely known to humans. We often think that iron and copper had the greatest impact on human progress - but gold came first. Gold was first discovered in its natural state, as shining, yellow nuggets, in streams all over the world. Gold neither corrodes nor tarnishes.

Gold is the easiest of the metals to work. It occurs in a pure and workable state. Most other metals tend to be found in ore-bodies that require smelting. Gold's early uses were no doubt ornamental, and its brilliance and permanence linked it to gods and royalty in early civilizations.

The earliest history of humans using gold has been lost, but its association with the gods, with immortality, and with wealth itself are common to many world cultures.

Gold is the basis of the jewellery industry. The quality of gold in jewellery can vary. The purity is measured in carats. Carats in gold jewellery refers to the amount of gold in the jewellery. The carat gold purity system is 24 based. 24 carat gold means pure gold. 12 carat gold would be 50 percent pure - 12 is half of 24. Pure gold is often referred to as 'fine gold'.

The purer the gold content in a piece of jewellery, the more valuable it is. Gold is often mixed with alloys, (metals, such as silver or nickel, added to strengthen the gold) to create more durable jewellery, particularly in gold rings and gold bracelets. 24 carat gold is too soft for most jewellery. Mixing other metals to create a gold alloy gives strength and hardness to gold jewellery. If you buy a gold object it will have a mark or stamp showing its purity.

18 carat gold ring with mark

Sources: http://www.onlygold.com/tutorialpages/historyfs.htm
http://sarit-jewelry.com/Info.html

Understanding Reports   Circle a letter or write an answer for questions 1 to 8.

1. What is known to be the first metal used by humans?
    A   iron   B   silver   C   gold   D   copper

2. A gold ring, described as being 12 carat gold would
    A   contain some impurities   B   be half gold and half of another metal
    C   not be given a purity stamp   D   be classified as 'fine gold'

3. What was the advantage of gold for ancient civilisations?
    A   it was found in the environment in its natural state
    B   it was more common than iron or copper
    C   it was the preferred metal of royalty and the gods
    D   it was readily strengthened with other metals

4. An advantage of using gold in jewellery is that it
    A   is a very soft metal
    B   does not corrode or tarnish
    C   can bring immortality
    D   is very expensive

5. A mark or stamp is added to gold objects to show that object's
    A   purity   B   weight   C   value   D   origin

6. What is a suitable replacement term for *durable* as it is used in the text?
    A   beautiful   B   expensive   C   lustrous   D   long-lasting

7. According to the text what is one metal mixed with gold to make an alloy?

    Write your answer on the line. _____

8. To change ores into metals, they must first be
    A   collected from streams
    B   heated and melted
    C   made into alloys
    D   given a stamp to show purity

Need to try another report? Check the contents page.

Lit Tip 15 – Improve your literacy skills   Abstract nouns

There are 4 types of nouns: common, proper, collective and abstract.
An **abstract** noun is an idea, emotion or feeling. It is **not** a physical object.
Your five senses cannot detect this group of nouns. You cannot see, hear, feel (touch), smell or taste these nouns.
Examples: love, fear, bravery, success, happiness, pride.
A number of abstract nouns end with ness: sadness, uselessness, fairness.

1. Underline the **abstract** nouns: song   hope   faith   air   test   leader   talent

2. Which abstract noun relates to something that has an attractive quality?
    b _ _ _ _ _ (5 more letters)

Understanding Year 5 Comprehension
A. Horsfield © Five Senses Education © W. Marlin

Bat-winged Cannibal Fly

Species details
Order: Diptera (meaning: two wings)
Common Names: Bat-winged fly,
Bat-winged cannibal fly

Description: A black fly, with broad, enlarged wings in the male, but not the female. The dark male wings are about 13mm long and 10mm wide. The thorax (body) has two distinct black stripes on a dark grey background.

Locality: Milford Sound, Fiordland, New Zealand

Fiordland National Park has spectacular ice-carved fiords, lakes, deep valleys, rugged granite peaks and glaciers. Seals laze on rocks along the fiord.

Fiordland NZ

Distribution: The fly may have a natural distribution from northern Fiordland to nearby ranges on the west coast. Since 1980 specimens have been collected from various places in the southern mountain range. The species' apparent rarity may be attributed to a lack of looking in the right places at the right time, and the inaccessibility of these alpine areas.

Habitat: It inhabits alpine meadows, particularly around streams. Often found sun-bathing on larger flat-topped lichen covered rocks in or beside streams. Specimens have been collected from altitudes between 760m and 1830m.

Bat-winged Cannibal Fly
The bat-winged cannibal fly is not only one of the most unusual insects in New Zealand. It is a very rare fly.
It is mostly found in the mountains sunning itself on a rock, its large black wings outspread to gather warmth from the sun. Once warm, the fly hunts along streams in search of prey, sucking moisture from the bodies of other insects caught on the wing.
This aptly named creature has previously been found at Milford Sound but little is known of its history. Like other predatory flies, it plays an important part in maintaining the delicate balance of nature.

Text from a display within Milford Sound ferry terminal.

Threats: It was thought to be endangered, but it is no longer listed as a threatened species. It is likely to be vulnerable to habitat degradation.

Source: http://www.doc.govt.nz/ documents/conservation/native-animals/ invertebrates/015-flies.pdf

Understanding Descriptions   Circle a letter or write an answer for questions 1 to 8.

1. The bat-winged cannibal fly is difficult to find mainly because it
   - A   lives in a remote area of high mountains
   - B   spends most of its time flying along streams
   - C   inhabits a small part of New Zealand
   - D   hides inside the Milford Sound ferry terminal

2. What does the name *Diptera* mean?
   Write your answer on the line.   _____

3. What is the cannibal fly's main source of food?
   - A   lichen from rocks
   - B   moisture sucked from insects
   - C   small stream animals
   - D   blood from seals

4. The bat-winged cannibal fly gets its warmth from
   - A   moisture taken from insects
   - B   hunting its prey
   - C   inside the ferry terminal
   - D   sun-bathing on rocks

5. The text states that the bat-winged cannibal fly catches prey *on the wing*. This term, *on the wing*, indicates that the cannibal fly
   - A   catches its prey while the prey is in flight
   - B   brings down its prey by attacking its wings
   - C   waits for prey to fly by
   - D   looks for prey on the wings of other insects

6. The two black stripes on the bat-winged cannibal fly are on its wings.

   Is this TRUE or FALSE? Tick a box.   TRUE ☐   FALSE ☐

7. Searchers for the cannibal fly are not sure how rare the fly is because they
   - A   experienced difficulties exploring rocky streams
   - B   may have looked in the wrong places
   - C   do not know about the fly's habitat and behaviour
   - D   have poor descriptions of the fly

8. What could a visitor to Milford Sound expect to see?
   - A   live bat-winged cannibal flies
   - B   seals in mountain streams
   - C   a ferry terminal
   - D   scientists collecting cannibal flies

Need to try another description? Check the contents page.

Understanding Year 5 Comprehension
A. Horsfield © Five Senses Education © W. Marlin

Gone Phishing

Both fishing and phishing (same pronunciation) are acts in which the goal is to catch prey. Unfortunately, internet users are the prey of phishers.

Phishing is similar to online email scams and viruses. The best defence is awareness.

What do they look like?

Phishing attempts often involve an email being sent, supposedly from a company that the recipient knows. The email asks the receiver to reveal personal details.

Phishing attempts include emails full of spelling mistakes, suspicious email addresses or very real looking emails with convincing signatures – that link to an authentic looking website. These catch people out!

A common phishing email looks as though it comes from a real company - with a scare tactic. For example: "For security reasons, you are required to prove your account validity by *clicking the following link* and logging in. Failure to do so will result in your account being shutdown."

A phishing email may look like this:

> Wesnet Support <john038@centurytel.net>
>
> To: undisclosed-recipients:Subject: Webmail at wrisk
>
> Your e-mail account is at wrisk. follow the link below and sign on resolving this error: https://webmail.wesnot.com.au// Failure to do this would lead to a suspension. Wesnot Support

Most people will instantly DELETE it, however some people will follow the instructions and unwittingly disclose login details and/or credit card details.

Phishing attempts are a nuisance and can be costly.

If you are too late in discovering something 'phishy' and have disclosed personal details:

- Change your password

- Inform your bank.

Adapted: Posted on March 8, 2013 by Chad Branks for Westnet

Understanding Explanations   Circle a letter or write an answer for questions 1 to 8.

1. The text, **Gone Phishing**, is written to
   - A   entertain the reader
   - B   provide a warning to the reader
   - C   frighten the reader
   - D   sell a product to the reader

2. What would a person do immediately after receiving a phishing email?
   - A   inform their bank
   - B   destroy their credit cards
   - C   delete the email
   - D   follow the given instructions

3. The *ph* in *phishing* makes an *f* sound
   Write another word in the box that has a *ph* sound as in *phishing*. ☐

4. The email in the box, in the centre of the text, is most likely a fake because it
   - A   went to the wrong email address
   - B   is not signed by any official
   - C   is full of spelling mistakes
   - D   does not have a webmail link

5. A suitable synonym for *authentic* would be
   - A   genuine   B   automatic   C   duplicate   D   legal

6. According to the text *'clicking the following link'* will mostly
   - A   lead to increased security of an email account
   - B   prevent an email account from being cancelled
   - C   provide the user with information on phishing
   - D   open a site designed to give access to personal details

7. Which word best describes the senders of phishing emails?
   - A   bold   B   deceitful   C   foolish   D   rude

8. What is the purpose of the scare tactic in a phishing email?
   - A   to frighten the receiver into making a rash decision
   - B   to alert the receiver that they may have a computer virus
   - C   to show the receiver how to download important information
   - D   to prepare the receiver for banking problems

Need to try another explanations? Check the contents page.

Lit Tip 17 – Improve your literacy skills   Using question marks

This **?** is a **question mark**. It's a form of punctuation that comes at the end of a sentence to show a question has been asked. Many words can be used to ask a question: how, when, where, why, what, will, are, is, do, can, could, should, would.

You can change a statement into a question by adding a question mark. It changes the way you say that statement. Different words are stressed.
Think about how you would say this: You are serious? It is said as if you don't believe what you have been told. Stress the word *are*. Try saying it aloud.

Make this statement sound like a question: The old man jumped the fence.
(Get someone to listen to how many ways you can say it to sound like different questions.)
A writing tip: Use question/statements in your writing to make the words your character says more interesting - don't do it too often!

Understanding Year 5 Comprehension
A. Horsfield © Five Senses Education © W. Marlin

The Final Kombi

They carried families on holidays, equipment for tradesmen, hippies in search of the perfect surf, summer after summer since 1950. The vast interior and flat roof were perfect for hauling surfboards. Kombis were the workhorses of people in the developing countries.

The long trip from 1950 came to an end on 31 December 2013. The VW Kombis, originally only produced in Germany, were produced in many other countries and production ended in Brazil. Over 10 million were produced in the 63 year history.

Safety regulations in Brazil required that every new vehicle in Brazil had to be equipped with air bags and anti-locking brakes from the beginning of 2014. The company couldn't change production to meet these requirements.

There are still plenty of Kombis around. They will be seen on the roads for decades because there are so many around and they are so _____(4)_____ and basic. They do break down but because the engine is so simple many owners could fix them.

The Kombi made appearances in films, in songs and on record covers. There are Kombi Clubs across Australia uniting enthusiasts who share the same interests. The Kombi Club has more than 10,000 members worldwide. The thing that remains the same from day one and that's the friendship, a willingness to help and the true Kombi spirit.

Kombi is an abbreviation for the German Kombinationsfahrzeug, meaning 'cargo-passenger van' which is what it was and how it was used!

Adapted from: Koolangat Tribune, Motoring Section January 2014

Understanding Reports   Circle a letter or write an answer for questions 1 to 8.

1. How many years was the VW Kombi in production?

    Write your answer in the box. ☐☐☐☐☐☐☐ years

2. Why did Brazil cease building Kombis?
    - A   new safety regulations increased production costs
    - B   production moved to the VW factory in Germany
    - C   Kombi developed a reputation for breaking down
    - D   they were no longer popular among tradesmen

3. The word *They* that begins paragraph 1 refers to
    - A   hippies   B   Kombi vans C   families   D   flat roofs

4. A word has been deleted from the text.
    Which word would be most suited to the space ___(4)___.
    - A   safe   B   faultless   C   sturdy   D   colourful

5. The reporter uses repetition when he writes: *summer* after *summer*
    The most likely reason for this repetition is that it
    - A   makes the point that hippies didn't like work
    - B   draws attention to the fact it was a very long time
    - C   indicates the reporter was unsure of his facts
    - D   suggests that the perfect surf took a long time to find

6. What is the most likely reason people join Kombi clubs?
    - A   help repair other members' Kombis
    - B   find where Kombis can be produced
    - C   share the workload of Kombi owners
    - D   enjoy the company of other Kombi owners

7. When did the last Kombi come off the production line?
    - A   1950   B   1963   C   2013   D   2014

8. What fact from the text most impressed the reporter?
    - A   the unity among Kombi owners   B   Brazil's Kombi safety regulations
    - C   Kombis have featured in films   D   Kombis never break down

Need to try another report? Check the contents page.

Lit Tip 18 – Improve your literacy skills   Analogies

An **analogy** is a comparison between one thing and another to make an explanation clear.
They are meant to improve communication.
If Dad said, "I feel like a fish out of water," this would imply Dad was not at ease.
Dad and the fish are alike in their distress.
Dad and the fish have this one shared characteristic.
Look at this analogy:
Dust is to rock as mist is to ice. (Dust and mist are air born particles of something solid.)

Circle the best word to complete this analogy.
Doors are to houses as (fences, gates, flowers) are to gardens.

Understanding Year 5 Comprehension
A. Horsfield © Five Senses Education © W. Marlin

The Microbe

The microbe is so very small
You cannot make him out at all,
But many sanguine* people hope
To see him through a microscope.

His jointed tongue that lies beneath
A hundred curious rows of teeth;
His seven tufted tails with lots
Of lovely pink and purple spots,
On each of which a pattern stands,
Composed of forty separate bands;
His eyebrows of a tender green;
All these have never yet been seen-
But Scientists, who ought to know,
Assure us that it must be so...

Oh! Let us never, never doubt
What nobody is sure about!

(*optimistic)

by: Hilaire Belloc (1870-1953)

"The Microbe" is reprinted from More Beasts for Worse Children. Hilaire Belloc. Duckworth, 1912.

http://www.poetry-archive.com/collections/poems_for_children.html

Understanding Poetry   Circle a letter to answer questions 1 to 8.

1. What is the colour of microbe's eyebrows?
    A   green   B   purple   C   pink   D   white

2. How does the narrator of the poem feel about the description of the microbe?
    A   it's factual   B   it's frightening
    C   it's unreliable   D   it's accurate

3. Which word from the poem rhymes with doubt?
    A   so   B   hope   C   beneath   D   about

4. Where are the forty bands of pattern on the microbe?
    A   on his tongue   B   on his tails
    C   on his teeth   D   on his body

5. The prefix *micro* in *microscope* means
    A   ugly   B   rare   C   small   D   savage

6. The poem is mainly
    A   a narrative   B   a description
    C   a recount   D   an explanation

7. As described in the poem, what is the gender of the microbe? (Check **Lit Tip 7** for 'gender')
    A   neuter   B   common   C   feminine   D   masculine

8. What does the narrator have doubts about?
    A   what scientists really know   B   the size of the microbe
    C   the colour of the microbe   D   if the microbe really exists

Need to try another poem? Check the contents page.

Understanding Year 5 Comprehension
A. Horsfield © Five Senses Education © W. Marlin

20 **Read the report *Origin of Tea*.**

Origin of Tea

- There are tales of tea's first use as a beverage, but no one is sure of its exact origins.

- According to legend, the first person to drink tea was a man named, Shien Non Shei, who one day took his wife and children mountain climbing. During the climb Shien Non Shei became quite thirsty. It was then a leaf drifted onto his foot. He picked this leaf up and twisted the leaf with his fingers. The juice of the leaf went onto his fingers and he tasted the juice. The juice was quite bitter, so Shien Non Shei felt that this leaf could have medicinal properties and could help quench thirst, when brewed. This was before 618 A.D.

- The first written reference of tea made and consumed appeared in 350 A.D. Kuo P'o' updated an old Chinese dictionary to include the description of tea as "a beverage made from boiled leaves." Tea, during this time, was made of leaves boiled in water with ginger, orange or other produce. Although tea was mostly consumed for medicinal purposes to treat digestive and nervous conditions, people living in the interior part of China used tea to barter with other tribes.

- From 350 to 600 A.D., the demand for tea increased and outstripped the supply of wild tea trees. Farmers began to grow tea plants in the Szechwan district, but soon tea cultivation spread across China.

- Tea was first introduced to Portuguese priests and merchants in China during the 16th century, at which time it was called chá.

- Tea is considered the favoured drink of the British!

Adapted from: http://www.tenren.com/teahistory.html

Understanding Reports   Circle a letter or write an answer for questions 1 to 8.

1. According to the text the first person to taste tea was
   A   Shien Non Shei   B   a Portuguese priest
   C   a farmer from Szechwan   D   Kuo P'o'

2. The history of tea drinking
   A   is of recent origins   B   goes back thousands of years
   C   began with the Portuguese   D   began with Kuo P'o's Chinese dictionary

3. Where was tea first planted as a crop?
   Write your answer on the line.   In _____

4. A legend is a
   A   traditional story thought of as history but may not be factual
   B   story that explains a natural event with supernatural forces
   C   story that provides a lesson on right and wrong behaviour
   D   short story involving animals with human characteristics

5. After he had tasted the bitter juice from the leaf Shien Non Shei
   A   crushed the leaf in his fingers
   B   replaced the leaf on his foot
   C   thought the leaf may have medical benefits
   D   gave the leaf to Portuguese merchants

6. According to the text, the people in the interior part of China used tea for
   A   the flavouring in fruit drinks   B   the exchange of goods
   C   medicinal purposes   D   pains in the fingers

7. In the text the word *consumed* refers to
   A   eating   B   drinking   C   healing   D   brewing

8. For what medicinal condition did the Chinese drink tea?
   A   hunger   B   exhaustion
   C   thirstiness   D   nervousness

Lit Tip 20 – Improve your literacy skills   Being precise (Check Lit Tip 12)

Using more precise words makes your writing more interesting and enjoyable.

Look at '*hit*' in this sentence: Anne <u>hit</u> the ball over the wall. *Hit* is an ordinary word.
The sentence changes meanings if *hit* is changed to tapped, chipped, sliced or belted.
Each one tells the reader something different about Anne.
Compare these *walk* words: hobble, stroll, amble, march, shuffle, skip, creep, crawl.

Suggest three better words than *ate* for this sentence: Grandpa ate his sausage.

_____   _____   _____

Understanding Year 5 Comprehension
A. Horsfield © Five Senses Education © W. Marlin

21 Read the explanation *Redundancies.*

Redundancies

Redundancy refers to using words which are unnecessary because they add nothing to the sense of the text.

A common example is at all: There was nobody there at all. *The words at all can be left out and the meaning does not change.*

Redundancy can involve one word or many words. Look at this sentence: *The reason I am fit is because I go to the gym.*

This could be more directly expressed by saying: *I am fit because I go to the gym.* Writers should go through their text and remove unnecessary words.

Examples of redundancies

1. The end result was a win for our boys.
   A result is something that occurs at the end. End can be omitted as a modifier of result.

2. The coach decided to postpone the training until later.
   To postpone is to put off until a time in the future. The use of until later is not needed.

Here are some commonly heard examples.

I use ATMs all the time but I call them Mum and Dad!

(advance) warning   (free) gift

(armed) gunman   (frozen) ice

cold (temperature)   green (in colour)

each (and every)   join (together)

boiling (hot)   (unexpected) surprise

Sometimes acronyms (words from initials) or just the initials contain redundancies.

ATM machine - machine is unnecessary
                - the M stands for machine

PIN (number)   HIV (virus)   GPS (public school)

Anyone can be guilty of using redundancies. An award-winning footballer has been reported saying: I want to thank my mother and father and my parents. (Really! Were they different people?)

Can you pick the redundancies in these sentences?

1. Sometimes you can observe a lot just by watching.
2. I never make predictions, especially about the future.

Understanding Explanations   Circle a letter to answer questions 1 to 8.

1. What is a feature of *redund*ancy in a sentence?
    A   common spelling mistakes   B   the repetition of information
    C   the incorrect use of verbs   D   exaggerating unnecessarily

2. What is wrong with saying a *free gift?*
    A   the gift might have to be paid for by the receiver
    B   some gifts are free and some are not
    C   a person getting a free gift knows it is a cheap gift
    D   if it is a gift then it's given freely

3. Which word is unnecessary in this sentence?
    The empty space was at the back of the drawer.
    A   empty   B   space   C   back   D   the

4. What is the correct option to fill the space in this sentence?
    Dad bought a _____ for us to watch.
    A   DVD disc   B   DV disc   C   DVD   D   DVDisc

5. The word *postpone* means to
    A   cancel an event   B   put off until later
    C   forfeit a game   D   cut short a competition

6. Which of these does **not** include a redundant word?
    A   repeat that again   B   a happy group of singers
    C   it is an annual anniversary   D   give her a bouquet of flowers

7. Which of these words from the text is a compound word?
    A   acronyms   B   surprise   C   postpone   D   gunman

8. Which verb will correctly complete this sentence?
    Mathematics _____ a headache every time I try to do long division.
    A   starts   B   make   C   begin   D   cause

Need to try another explanation? Check the contents page.

Lit Tip 21 – Improve your literacy skills   **Singular nouns that look like plurals**

There are nouns that look as if they are plural nouns but they are singular nouns.
Examples: news, politics, economics, physics, mathematics, Philippines.
Many fall into groups; Activities: athletics, gymnastics.
                        Games: billiards, cards, darts, Olympics.
                        Diseases: mumps, measles, rabies.
Complete these with singular verbs.

1. Dominoes _____ played at home last night.

2. Aerobics _____ held daily.

3. Bowls _____ cancelled after the storm.

4. Brussels _____ the capital city of Belgium.

Understanding Year 5 Comprehension
A. Horsfield © Five Senses Education © W. Marlin

(You may have completed an earlier text on Christmas Lights in text No. 3. This one provides another point of view.)

Austin Marsh wrote this about decorating houses with Christmas lights.

Christmas Lights (2)

Do we really need huge displays of Christmas lights for private homes?

Most people are not against decorations at Christmas time or any other time as long as they kept within reason. What I dislike are whole homes and yards done up like sideshow alley. These displays are now excessive expressions of consumerism.

Christmas lights are becoming unhealthy competitions between neighbours, streets and suburbs. It's a case of 'anything you can do I can do better' regardless of cost. The retailers must be smiling all the way to the bank. Christmas comes once a year!

In some cases there is a safety factor for the parents who climb onto rooftops to create their shows. How often do we hear of falls from roofs or ladders and people fooling unnecessarily with electricity and, no doubt, overloading a multitude of power outlets?

But what does the visitor to the street get to see? To me it's not pretty and has little to do with the real meaning behind Christmas.

There is no place for plastic blow-up Santas, reindeers bouncing across roof ridges or garish lights flashing incessantly. These distract drivers who have come to gawk at the displays creating congestion on suburban streets and accidents caused by Christmas lights!

Worst of all is the unnecessary waste of a scarce resource – electricity from pollution creating power stations. In a time of global shortages is this what we want Australia to be famous for? Let's do away with the big displays and get Christmas back inside the home with the family.

Austin Marsh
(Adapted from an unknown source.)

Understanding Persuasions   Circle a letter to answer questions 1 to 8.

1. Which option best describes how Austin feels about Christmas light decorations?
    Austin feels Christmas lights are

    A   an unnecessary extravagance   B   not important to children
    C   a welcome sight for drivers   D   an essential part of Christmas

2. According to the writer, what is the worst thing about Christmas lights?

    A   the accidents when people fall off ladders or off roofs
    B   the unnecessary expense to families
    C   the overloading of the power supply
    D   the waste of power from polluting power stations

3. According to Austin who gets the most benefit from Christmas lights?

    A   bankers   B   neighbourhood visitors
    C   power suppliers   D   Christmas light retailers

4. Austin describes Christmas lights as being *garish*.
    Garish lights are ones that are

    A   artificial   B   annoying   C   showy   D   coloured

5. Austin believes that Christmas lights should be

    A   banned totally   B   kept inside the family home
    C   put up by electricians   D   cost much less

6. Which of the following sentences from the text is an opinion?

    A   There is a safety factor for the parents who climb onto rooftops.
    B   Most people are not against decorations at Christmas time.
    C   Christmas comes once a year.
    D   There is no place for plastic blow-up Santas.

7. Which word best describes how Austin feels about houses covered in Christmas lights?

    A   excited   B   dismayed   C   confused   D   frustrated

8. The text begins with a question. The purpose of this question is to

    A   get readers to provide an answer   B   test readers on their knowledge
    C   arouse the reader's interest   D   prevent accidents at home

---

Lit Tip 22 – Improve your literacy skills   Word Building

Prefixes and suffixes create new words by modifying or changing the meaning.
The word *kind*, can be given the opposite meaning with the prefix *un* (unkind).
Unkind can be turned into an adverb by adding the suffix *ly* (unkindly).
Other words can be added to *way*: highwayman. This is a compound word.

Some words built from *set* include:
sets, setting, settle, settler, unsettled, inset, reset, setback, typesetter, sunset, setup

Build your own words with *know*: _____ _____ _____

Understanding Year 5 Comprehension
A. Horsfield © Five Senses Education © W. Marlin

How to Whistle

A whistle is a clear, high-pitched sound made by forcing breath through a small hole between partly closed lips, or between one' rshing s teeth. Whistling came before musical instruments.

Anyone can whistle. Just purse your lips and blow. Sounds easy, but like tying shoes or riding a bike, whistling is one of those skills adults take for granted. Whether we do it to call the dog or pass the time, we give the art of whistling little thought.

For many of us, this talent didn't develop overnight. We did not learn to whistle in tune without hard work, frustration and exhaling until we were blue in the face.

There are many whistling styles, including tongue and palate, finger and hand. The most common, and easiest to learn is the pucker whistle.

Some tips for learning the **pucker whistle**

1. Practice in front of a mirror.

2. Before you begin, lick your lips to make them moist.

3. Say "ooh," to check the position of your mouth. The lips should form a small circle. The tongue should be slightly curled. Either press the tongue against the bottom teeth or hold it slightly back.

4. Without blowing too hard, gently blow a steady stream of air through the small opening of the lips. You can try sucking the air in.

5. Adjust the position of the lips and tongue until they produce a note.

The trick is to keep practising. If you can't make a note, keep going until you get a note and then figure out how you made that note. Keep whistling until you can do it at will, because the first time is likely to be an accident. Soon you'll be whistling like a bird - or a kettle!

Adapted from: http://www.metroparent.com/Metro-Parent/December-2012/
Teaching-Kids-How-to-Whistle/

Understanding Procedures   Circle a letter or write an answer for questions 1 to 8.

1. For most children learning to whistle
    A   can be frustrating   B   is as simple as breathing
    C   requires an expert teacher   D   can be achieved quickly

2. Children who have difficulties learning to whistle should
    A   give up trying   B   watch how birds whistle
    C   wait until they get older   D   keep practising

3. According to the text to make a whistle: *Just <u>purse</u> your lips and blow.*
    What part of speech is purse in this sentence?
    A   noun   B   verb   C   adverb   D   preposition

4. The writer says when you start whistling you might sound like *a kettle.*
    When he says this he means you
    A   are whistling a melody   B   are making a hissing sound
    C   whistling without any tune   D   whistling better than a song bird

5. Write the numbers 1 to 4 in the boxes to show the order of things you must do to be able to whistle.
    The first one (1) has been done for you.

☐	say "ooh" to get your mouth the right shape
☐	adjust the position of the tongue and lips until you get a whistle
1	moisten your lips using your tongue
☐	gently blow a stream of air

6. As used in the text, the phrase *until we were blue in the face* means
    A   trying something repeatedly
    B   about to die from lack of air
    C   being in a poor medical state
    D   having our faces painted blue

7. When a person exhales they are
    A   suffocating   B   breathing out   C   panting   D   feeling exhausted

8. The text **How to Whistle** is written in which tense? (You can check **Lit Tip 10** for tense)
    A   past tense   B   present tense   C   future tense

Need to try another procedure? Check the contents page.

Lit Tip 23 – Improve your literacy skills   **Onomatopoeia**
                                    (Pronounced: ono -mata- **pee** -ah)
Onomatopoeia refers to a word that sounds like the sound it represents, e.g. hiss.
Many animal noises are examples of this: meow, honk, squawk, baa, chirp.
Using onomatopoeia carefully can make your writing more interesting.

Compare: Water <u>boiled</u> on the stove.   Water <u>bubbled</u> on the stove.
          Sausages <u>fried</u> in the pan.   Sausages <u>sizzled</u> in the pan.

Add suitable 'sound' verbs: Little bells _____, Explosions _____

Understanding Year 5 Comprehension
A. Horsfield © Five Senses Education © W. Marlin

Read the review of an educational facility - *Tokaanu Thermal Walk*.

Tokaanu Thermal Walk (NZ)

The thermal walk takes 20 minutes - with a group of students, longer time is required for explanations. The walk around the pools is set up as an education facility for students of all grades. It passes through an area of hot springs, which have been used by the Maori people for 500 years for baking and cooking food. The Maoris also recognised the health properties of the mineral waters.

The water first fell as rain or snow and eventually seeped deep below the surface and came in contact with hot volcanic rock. It is driven back to the surface where it emerges as steam and hot thermal springs rich in minerals.

Along the way students see spluttering, boiling mud ponds, pools bubbling with hot water, steam hissing from rocky vents and small warm, clear water streams.

Between the points of interest are wide, firm paths and ample warnings to stay on the paths.

Features are visually interesting - with a whiff of sulphur. This is not dangerous and not really unpleasant.

There are many places along the path that are not fenced, however where pools are close to the path, sturdy fences make viewing safe. In unfenced sections there is ample scrub to deter any attempt to leave the formed track. Boardwalks by steaming ponds and over streams are well fenced.

Teacher knowledge is essential if maximum benefit is to be gained from the excursion. The site would benefit from information boards next to the various sites. This could include some information on Maori culture and the temperature in some of the thermal features. The removal of branches overhanging some of the lookout points would make viewing more accessible.

Educational rating: 4 / 5

Accessibility rating: 5 / 5

Cost: Free

Understanding Reviews   Circle a letter to answer questions 1 to 8.

1. What must students visiting the Tokaanu Thermal Walk do?
    A   stay on the formed tracks
    B   respect Maoris using the pools for cooking
    C   complete the walk in 20 minutes
    D   avoid breathing the sulphur fumes

2. Which word best describes the reviewer's opinion of the thermal walk?
    A   dangerous   B   exhausting   C   worthwhile   D   unpleasant

3. Which word from the text is an example of onomatopoeia? (See **Lit Tip 23**)
    A   whiff   B   hiss   C   steaming   D   mineral

4. What does the reviewer feel is a shortcoming of the facility as a school excursion?
    A   the distance of the walk   B   the possibility of an accident
    C   the unpleasant sulphur smell   D   the lack of readily available information

5. The viewing of some of the thermal features is made difficult because of
    A   overhanging vegetation
    B   Maoris using the pools
    C   lack of safety fences
    D   rising steam

6. What must a teacher do to prepare for a class visit to Tokaanu Thermal Walk?
    A   make sure the students can read the warning signs
    B   understand the features of the thermal walk
    C   have sufficient money for the entry fee
    D   provide gas masks for students

7. How does the reviewer rate the location as an educational opportunity?
    A   poor   B   adequate   C   average   D   good

8. Students visiting the Tokaanu Thermal Walk should expect to feel
    A   scared   B   warm   C   exhausted   D   refreshed

Lit Tip 24 – Improve your literacy skills   **Alliteration**

Alliteration is the use of the same letter or sound at the beginning of words that are close together in the text: rugged rocks, chocolate chips.

Alliteration can add interest to your writing.
Underline the letters that are used for alliteration in these examples.
1. misty mountains   2. Twelve little twins   3. filthy fish fingers

Here are some family names. Use alliteration to add a first name (e.g. Jack Jones).

1. _____ Bolt, 2. _____ Turner, 3. _____ Pope, 4. _____ Heron

Understanding Year 5 Comprehension
A. Horsfield © Five Senses Education © W. Marlin

Where in Australia?

A B Patterson suggested in a poem that there was a town worse than Hay or Hell - it was Booligal. Hay and Booligal exist but to suggest there was a town called Hell was an invention. However, a quick Google check revealed a few places in Australia called Hells Gate.

So, if you cannot live in Hell can you live in Paradise?

Journalist, Sue Webster, has done some research on the subject. Here's what she had to say:

> *"I've seen Paradise. It has a landing strip.*
> *If you are seeking the ultimate in spiritual <u>ecstasy</u>, it's reassuring to know you can get there by Cessna.*
> *Actually it's the only NSW Paradise that has a landing strip.*
> *Another one in North Adelaide has a bus interchange.*
> *A third one appears to be a junkyard near Dardanup West (WA).*
> *I never knew Paradise came with a postcode: 3381 if you're a Victorian, or 7360 if you're a Tasmanian. It's 2360 if you want your Paradise with a landing strip or 5070 if you're bus-bound."*

In Queensland you can live at Surfers Paradise (4217), Paradise Point (4216) or on Paradise Island on the Gold Coast. Paradise Dam is on the Burnett River.

Unfortunately there is nowhere in the Postcode book called Heaven but there is a place called Hope and another called the Plains of Promise but no Promised Land. Eden is on the NSW South Coast - near Palestine.

Personally I'd be happy living in Snug (Tas), or in Sunshine in a choice of states, all with postcodes.

Inspired by an idea from: Heaven is a place on Earth Sue Webster Air North 2012 Feb/March.

Understanding Reports   Circle a letter or write an answer for questions 1 to 8.

1. This report is most likely intended to

    A   guide the reader   B   educate the reader

    C   confuse the reader   D   amuse the reader

2. Who wrote about Hell being a town a little better than Booligal? (Tick a box.)

    A B Patterson ☐   Sue Webster ☐

3. What is a synonym for *ecstasy* as used by the quoted writer Sue Webster?

    A   bliss   B   success   C   excitement   D   hope

4. As a writer, Sue Webster's descriptions of Paradise is intended to be

    A   serious   B   humiliating   C   light-hearted   D   hilarious

5. According to the text, if you live in a place called *Sunshine*

    A   the weather is mostly fine

    B   it could be in a number of different states

    C   you might find it doesn't have a postcode

    D   it is the best place to live in

6. The text reveals that Australian place names

    A   are unique   B   are unremarkable

    C   describe their location   D   can be surprising

7. The writer most likely thinks living in Snug would be

    A   exciting   B   cosy   C   lonely   D   sunny

8. A suitable alternative title for the passage would be

    A   Postcodes for Paradise   B   The road to Booligal

    C   From Eden to Palestine   D   Look for a signpost

Need to try another report? Check the contents page.

Lit Tip 25 – Improve your literacy skills   **Comparative adjectives**

Adjectives are often referred to as describing words, e.g. <u>happy</u> child, <u>broken</u> toy.
Now look at *hot, hotter* and *hottest*. <u>One</u> tap is <u>hot</u>. Comparing <u>two</u> taps, one is <u>hotter</u> than the other. Comparing <u>many</u> taps, one is the <u>hottest</u> of all the taps.
Do you see the pattern? The base word (hot) describes one tap. The suffix *er* compares **two** taps. The suffix *est* compares **three** or more (many) taps.
Comparing adjectives using *slow* (base word): slow (1), slower (2), slowest (3 +).

For words with many syllables the pattern changes a bit.
Take *beautiful*: We don't say beautifuller or beautifullest. They are **wrong!**
We say; beautiful (1), <u>more</u> beautiful (2), <u>most</u> beautiful (3 +)
Using the above pattern complete these groups of comparative adjectives

new (1), _____ (2) _____ (3 +);

interesting (1) _____ (2) _____ (3 +).

Understanding Year 5 Comprehension
A. Horsfield © Five Senses Education © W. Marlin

Read the narrative *The Fly Trap.*

The Fly Trap

One day a deliveryman came to the shop pushing a trolley. He had some new plants for Venuti's Flower Shop.

Lorenzo watched his mother place the small pot plants in her shop window. There were little cacti with funny shapes and colours, African violets, and some really strange plants.

Lorenzo read one of the tags.

Venus Fly Trap
Carnivorous Plant
Sunny, damp position best.
Grows to 4 or 5 cm.
Venuti's Flower Shop   2 Euros

'What about those?' his mother called. 'They eat animals!'

Lorenzo frowned. Plants eating animals! That's different.

'Well, insects at least!' added his mother.

When he looked carefully he could see the plant had small jaw-like traps that could snap shut on unsuspecting insects. Insects were hardly real animals, he thought. Not like tigers and bears.

'You can have one, if you like. As long as you care for it,' his mother offered.

Lorenzo chose one in a ceramic pot. He carried it as if it were a fluffy chick. He put his plant on his windowsill that overlooked the piazza. The fly traps were no bigger than his little fingernail.

He watched his plant for a while hoping to see some action, but no insects came anywhere close. He even tried to find some flies or ants to feed his plant but without success.

Maybe if he went out into the piazza he might find a small mouse sleeping in a sunny corner.

Lorenzo looked at his plant and shook his head. Unfortunately, a mouse would be much too large. He'd leave the mice to Gladiator!

Finally, he got tired of waiting and went downstairs and into the piazza for something better to do. Lorenzo spent much of his time hanging out there, and watching what went on – especially watching Mrs Bellini's cat, Gladiator - when it wasn't watching him!

The cat didn't like him – and the feeling was mutual.

Understanding Narratives Circle a letter to answer questions 1 to 8.

1. What did Lorenzo try to find to feed his plant?
   A a mouse   B a cat   C a bear   D an ant

2. The writer completes the text with: *the feeling was mutual.*
   This tells the reader that Lorenzo and Gladiator
   A behaved like mutants
   B shared the same dislike of each other
   C made friends very easily
   D had mixed feeling about each other

3. Which word would best describe Lorenzo's character?
   A thoughtful   B nervous   C excitable   D distrustful

4. Which option has the correct sequence of things Lorenzo did?
   After Lorenzo's mother received the Venus fly traps in her shop, Lorenzo
   A was given a plant, took the plant to his room, looked for insects, went to the piazza
   B looked for insects, was given a plant, took the plant to his room, went to the piazza
   C went to the piazza, looked for insects, was given a plant, took the plant to his room
   D was given a plant, went to the piazza, looked for insects, took the plant to his room

5. One possible reason Lorenzo put his fly trap on the window sill was because it
   A was safe from cats   B would not be seen by Mrs Bellini
   C would attract mice   D was a sunny position

6. Which of these lines from the text is an example of a simile?
   A as if it were a fluffy chick
   B there were little cacti with funny shapes and colours
   C Not like tigers and bears.
   D Lorenzo spent much of his time hanging out there

7. The text is written in
   A first person   B second person   C third person

8. When Lorenzo was first told about the Venus fly traps he was
   A amazed   B unbelieving C disinterested D cautious

Need to try another narrative? Check the contents page.

Lit Tip 26 – Improve your literacy skills   **Euphemisms**

A **euphemism** is a nice way of saying something that may be considered unpleasant or embarrassing. We say someone *passed away* instead of saying *died*.
If something *fell off the back of a truck* it usually means it *was stolen!*
If someone is *between jobs* it means they are *out of work*.
One way of saying something can be less upsetting than another way.

Complete these with a more direct word. 1. A *preloved* car is a _____ car.
Euphemisms aren't always polite. 2. *Kicked the bucket* means someone _____.

Understanding Year 5 Comprehension
A. Horsfield © Five Senses Education © W. Marlin

Comic Strips

A comic strip is a sequence of drawings or graphics, arranged in panels or frames. They display brief humour or form a narrative (often serialised), with the spoken words in balloons (or speech bubbles). Comics often have a caption.

Traditionally, throughout the 20th century and into the 21st, comics were published in daily newspapers with horizontal strips printed in black-and-white, while Sunday newspapers offered longer sequences in a colour comics section.

Strips are written and drawn by a comic artist or cartoonist although recently they have become known as graphic artists.

Comic Strip 1

Comic Strip 2

Note: a padre is a chaplain in the armed forces

Comic strips from: http://www.freechristianillustrations.com/cartoons.html
Text source: http://en.wikipedia.org/wiki/Comic_strip

Understanding comic strips   Circle a letter or write an answer for questions 1 to 8.

1. How many frames in each comic strip? Write your answer in the box. ☐

2. **Comic Strip 1** is amusing because
   - A   it relies on a double meaning for the word *cross*
   - B   the padre becomes unexpectedly aggressive
   - C   the characters have funny facial expressions
   - D   the padre wears his cross all the time

3. An alternative word for *graphics* as used in the text would be
   - A   symbols   B   conversations   C   illustrations   D   characters

4. What do symbols like these in comic strips usually represent ✳!@★
   - A   a foreign language   B   incorrect grammar
   - C   jumbled words   D   vulgar words

5. Which would be a suitable caption to go above **Comic Strip 2?**
   - A   Fishing is better than cricket   B   An acceptable explanation?
   - C   Fishermen's stories   D   Is it a secret?

6. Graphic artists have ways of showing different things.
   What is the artist showing here?
   - A   violent action
   - B   two people close together
   - C   getting a headache
   - D   sudden movement

7. Which face best expresses embarrassment?
   A   B   C   D

8. **Comic Strip 2** is amusing because the
   - A   boy's excuse misses the point   B   minister is easily fooled
   - C   minister doesn't believe the boy   D   boy is telling a lie

---

Lit Tip 27 – Improve your literacy skills   Writing addresses

We are still required to send mail, especially official or important documents. There is a 'correct' way to address the envelope.

Top line: Person's name (or official title)	Mr L Gold ☐	(no comma after name)
Second Line: Street number and name	77 Mineshaft St	(no full stop for St)
(or Post Office Box number)	(or PO Box 231)	(no full stops for PO)
Third line: Town/ suburb	Quarryland	
Fourth Line: State (using 2/3 capitals)	QLD 4999	(Post code included)

On a piece of paper write your own address. Keep each new line in line (don't slope).
Note: Don't include any punctuation unless it's essential.

Understanding Year 5 Comprehension
A. Horsfield © Five Senses Education © W. Marlin

Summer Fun

Characters: Mum, Dad and their children, Talia, Stella and Mark.

Scene: A family kitchen

Mum	If you are going outside to play you must wear a hat.
Mark:	If I have to wear a hat I'll wear my beanie!
Talia:	That's no good. It has to have a broad brim.
Dad:	And you'll need some sunscreen.
Mark:	Yuk, yuk, yuk.
Talia:	My teacher said it will stop you getting cancer. It's the first rule for playing in the sun.
Stella:	Not really. Slip is first. You slip on protective clothing then you slop on the sunscreen.
Dad:	Does the order really matter?
Stella:	It is easier to put on sunscreen on before you put on your hat.
Mark:	What about the hat?
Stella:	That comes next. Slap on a hat.
Mum:	That sounds right. Slip, slop, slap! Excellent.
Dad:	Then you can go outside and play.
Talia:	The sunscreen has to be the right strength! To stop the UV rays.
Mark:	What's UV?
Talia:	It's, it's . . .
Stella:	It's the ultra violet rays. The ones you can't see!
Mark:	Then they won't hurt me! I'm off.
Mum:	Only when you've done the slip, slop, slap bit.
Stella:	Not true Mum.
Talia:	Of course it is.
Dad:	Please explain.
Stella:	You still have to do seek and slide. (She smirks at Mark.)
Mum:	Seek and slide?
Stella:	Seek shade and slide on some sunglasses.
Mark:	All this just to go out and play. Too much!
Dad:	It's for your own good. (Mark turns around to leave the stage.)
Mum:	Where are you going Mark? (Mark turns back to face the family)
Mark:	I'm going to my room to play games. It's too much of a hassle to go outside!

Understanding Play Scripts   Circle a letter to answer questions 1 to 8.

1. The action of the play take place
    A   in a bedroom   B   at a school
    C   at the beach   D   in a kitchen

2. Of all the characters which one seems to know the most about sun protection?
    A   Mum   B   Dad   C   Stella   D   Talia

3. According to Talia, which would be the best hat for a sunny day?

    A   B   C   D

4. You read that Stella *smirks* at Mark. A smirk is a
    A   happy, cheerful smile   B   smug, irritating smile
    C   wide, radiant smile   D   quick, cruel smile

5. Who knew what UV rays were?
    A   Mark   B   Dad   C   Talia   D   Stella

6. Which statement shows how Mark felt about being sun safe?
    A   He was happy knowing he could be sun safe.
    B   He realised it made playing in the sun more fun.
    C   He felt it interfered with what he really wanted to do.
    D   He was eager to learn more about being sun safe.

7. The words, *slip, slop and slap,* are an example of
    onomatopoeia   alliteration   rhyme   a euphemism
    (Check **Lit Tip 23**)   (Check **Lit Tip 24**)   (Check **Lit Tip 26**)
    A   B   C   D

8. A suitable alternate title for the play could be
    A   Too much advice!   B   Slip, slop, slap
    C   Happy families   D   Mark plays games

Lit Tip 28 – Improve your literacy skills   Non-sentences

We usually think we should use a complete sentence in our narrative writing.
Using non-sentences is a writing tool just like using similes. Compare these two lines.
1. Around the corner cruised a big black car and it came to a stop outside our bank.
2. Around the corner cruised a car. Big and black. It stopped. Outside our bank.
The second example adds more tension and mystery to the text.

Non-sentences can make writing more exciting. They increase the pace.
Example: Ned heard a shot. Then another. He looked left. Right and up. Then listened.

Note: Non-sentences are an effective writing technique - but don't use them too often!

Understanding Year 5 Comprehension
A. Horsfield © Five Senses Education © W. Marlin

The Humble Spade

The spade is the gardener's best friend. Every garden begins with a spade. A good garden spade can cut through soil like butter, break up clods, pry stones, trim sods, divide perennials, chop roots, slice weeds and decapitate slugs. The one task it's not meant for is scooping loose material like gravel that calls for a shovel, which has a concave blade.

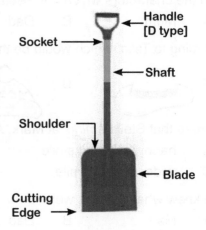

Grip: This can be a T shape but is usually D-shaped. With the YD shape, the handle is split and curved up to form the sides of the grip. Wooden grips are traditional, metal ones wear well but are heavier and plastic is waterproof but hard on the hands.

Handle: Generally made of hardwood. Handles are sometimes fashioned from tubular metal for heavy-duty work, or from fibreglass, which is lighter. Wear gloves when working with a fibreglass handle to prevent blisters.

Tread: The 'shoulders' of the blade have little metal platforms that act as foot treads. Sturdy treads may prevent your foot from slipping off.

Blade: This may be forged of carbon steel, which is strong and inexpensive, or stainless steel, which is shiny, rustproof and more expensive. The key is how the blade is attached to the handle – by a socket or by straps that extend up the handle. Straps are stronger but, should the handle break, socketed spades are easier to repair. Use a file to keep the blade sharp.

Remember, a quality spade will be a friend for life.

Sources: By Karen York http://www.gardeninglife.ca/articles/article/parts-spade/
http://sacredhabitats.com/2011/04/07/selecting-and-using-tools-shovels/

Understanding Descriptions   Circle a letter or write an answer for questions 1 to 8.

1. A spade is not a suitable tool to

   A   break up clods of dirt   B   scoop up gravel

   C   pry loose stones   D   chop through roots

2. Where on a spade are its shoulders?

   A   on top of the handle

   B   where the handle meets the shaft

   C   on the top side of the blade

   D   at the cutting edge of the blade

3. The text, *The humble Spade*, is factual or fictional?

   Tick a box.   Factual ☐   Fictional ☐

4. The word *decapitate* is applied to slugs. To *decapitate* is to

   A   capture   B   collect   C   remove   D   behead

5. Which handle shape is the most usual for spades?

   A   Y   B   D   C   ▽   D   T

6. A person should wear gloves when using a spade with a

   A   fibreglass handle   B   T shaped handle

   C   split handle   D   tubular metal handle

7. How would the writer treat a spade?

   A   as having little worth   B   easily replaced

   C   with respect   D   as a very ordinary tool

8. Stainless steel blades have an advantage over other blade types because they

   A   have a safer shoulder   B   are easily attached to the handle

   C   cannot be damaged   D   are not going to rust

Need to try another script? Check the contents page.

Lit Tip 29 – Improve your literacy skills   The prefix *a*

We often forget that the letter *a* can be a prefix. As a prefix *a* has a variety of meanings.
Usually it relates to the way things happen: aloud, afoot, asleep.
It can relate to a position: aside, aloft, away, ahead, aboard.
It may mean *on* or *in*: abed, aground, abroad.
It can mean *not* as in atypical (not typical).

Use the *a* prefix to describe something that is:
floating _____, living _____, on the shore _____.

Remember: The *a* is **not** a prefix in many words! For example: atom, amen, acorn.

Understanding Year 5 Comprehension
A. Horsfield © Five Senses Education © W. Marlin

The Editor,
Daily Torch
29-31 Bright Street
Glowtown 2889

They are popping up in shopping malls! What? Machines that dispense videos!

Now, there is nothing wrong with machines that dispense goods. We get chips, drinks, ice, and cash from vending machines. Shopping areas abound with vending machines.

We all saw the problem with cigarette machines. Children had easy, unsupervised access to cigarettes without going into a shop. Shops had restrictions on who could purchase such items.

What is so wrong with renting a video from a vending machine? I believe they are a bit like the cigarette machines. Underage people have access to films that may be M, AO or R rated. A credit card is required, but under 18s can have a credit card - and an email address to get the payment receipt. It's too easy for the underage to bypass scrutiny.

With 'R' rated films in cinemas young adults have to produce an ID card. Research shows that watching such movies without parent/adult supervision will lead children into accepting, swearing, drugs and violent behaviour as normal behaviour!

Who is standing beside a video dispensing machine to monitor what a juvenile takes from the machine? No ID check here! I can imagine children renting an inappropriate movie and taking it home to view while their parents are absent.

Maybe they watch their illicit video with younger brothers and sisters or young friends. The value has gone from movie ratings.

Ratings were intended to safeguard the young from exposures to the worst aspects of life.

_____(8)_____

Yours sincerely,

Tessa Raymer

Understanding Letter to an Editor Circle a letter to answer questions 1 to 8.

1. What is the main complaint in Tessa's letter to the editor of the *Daily Torch?*
   Her main complaint is about
   - A children misusing credit cards for purchases
   - B cigarettes available from cigarette machines
   - C unsupervised access to video rentals
   - D the range of items that are dispensed in machines

2. The first paragraph of Tessa's letter is intended to
   - A upset the reader
   - B encourage the reader to read on
   - C persuade the editor to print her letter
   - D make mall owners aware of a vending machine problem

3. What is the function of a *vending machine?*
   - A to dispense small articles
   - B to give people something to do
   - C to save shoppers time
   - D to avoid laws that protect children

4. Which of these words from the text uses *a* as a prefix? (Check **Lit Tip 29**)
   - A areas
   - B abound
   - C adult
   - D access

5. Tessa asks: *What is so wrong with renting a video from a vending machine?*
   By asking this question she
   - A expects to get information
   - B is accusing venders of videos of fraud
   - C is confused about her facts
   - D is trying to arouse the reader's interest

6. Which option best describes Tessa's general reaction to vending machines?
   - A they can be useful
   - B they cause problems for families
   - C they interfere with shopping
   - D they should be banned

7. If an item is *illicit* it is
   - A private
   - B afflicted
   - C illegal
   - D illiterate

8. The last line has been deleted from Tessa's letter.
   What would be a suitable concluding statement for the space (8)?
   - A Under 18s should have the same rights as adults.
   - B The government should protect children from drugs.
   - C There are too many vending machines.
   - D Video vending machines should be removed from shopping malls.

Lit Tip 30 – Improve your literacy skills   Persuasive text words

Persuasive writing has to be 'strong' if it is to convince someone else of what you say
is important. The writer must express opinions firmly. Here are some useful words:
I believe, In my opinion, Anyone can see, Research shows, It's a fact, Most importantly

Words such as *may, maybe, it seems, it could be, I suppose, I understand,* and *I reckon*
do not convince the reader or inspire confidence.
Instead of beginning a sentence with *I think,* try something stronger, such as *I know.*
It is important to be **positive**.

Understanding Year 5 Comprehension
A. Horsfield © Five Senses Education © W. Marlin

Land Sailing

Land Sailing is the sport of moving across land in a three-wheeled vehicle powered by wind through the use of a sail. It's like water sailing. Originally land sailing was used as a transport method. Since the ____(6)____ it has become a racing sport.

Land sailboats function much like a sailing boat except that they are operated from a sitting or lying position and steered by pedals or levers. Land sailing works best in windy, flat areas, and races often take place on dry lakebeds in desert regions. Land sailors can go three to four times faster than the wind speed.

The forces at work are the same as in water sailing, but the results are different because the conditions are different. Forces make things move, and forces can slow or stop moving objects. In sailing, the main force causing motion is the push of the wind on the sail. The force holding back a water sailboat is the friction of the water on the hull.

Land sailboats can go faster because their wheels have much less friction on dry surfaces than boats do in water.

The remote Lake Leroy is a large, usually dry, salt lake in Western Australia south of Kalgoorlie. It is considered by many to be one of the best places in the world to sail a land craft due to its size and the texture of its flat, smooth surface.

An attempt at the world land speed record at Lake Leroy failed in 2008. Mother Nature failed to help out. A world land speed record of 203 km/h was set in Nevada (USA) in 2009.

Adapted from: http://pierretorset.photoshelter.com/image/I0000I7zm2Go1IAw http://en.wikipedia.org/wiki/Land_sailing

Understanding Explanations   Circle a letter to answer questions 1 to 8.

1. Originally land sailing was

A   an opportunity to test water sailing skills

B   used as a method to transport goods

C   a competitive speed sport

D   used to break land sailing records

2. A possible disadvantage of Lake Leroy as a site for land sailing records is the

A   lack of suitable winds   B   quality of the salt surface

C   extreme flatness of the lakebed   D   isolation of the site

3. Choose the word from the text that is a compound word.

A   surface   B   originally   C   lakebeds   D   transport

4. For what reason is land sailing faster than water sailing?

A   tyres have less surface friction than boat hulls

B   water sailing uses smaller sails than land sailing

C   the wind at sea is not as strong as wind across land

D   sailors on land can operate their craft from a sitting position

5. What is implied by the sentence: *Mother Nature failed to help out?*

A   no one came along to help   B   Mother Nature is unreliable

C   there was insufficient wind   D   the weather reports were incorrect

6. A word has been deleted from the text.
Which option is correct for the space (6)?

A   1950's   B   1950S   C   1950ies   D   1950s

7. There are two forces affecting the speed of a sea sailboat or land sailboat.
These forces are wind strength and

A   weather conditions   B   surface friction

C   race regulations   D   the sailor's position in the craft

8. It is likely the wind speed on the day the land speed record was made (2009) was

A   about 203 km/h   B   greater than 203 km/h

C   a little less than 203 km/h   D   much less than 203 km/h

---

Lit Tip 31 – Improve your literacy skills   Brackets

Brackets are a form of punctuation. They are used to enclose extra information that the reader may find interesting or clarifies a point the writer is making. In many ways they are short cuts to providing additional information.

Examples:

1. Mary Hoxon (1963–2013) wrote seven novels. The dates in brackets indicate when Mary lived.
2. Snowy River wattle (*Acacia boormanii*) grows in NSW. The writer has provided the scientific name in brackets – and italics.

Removing the words in brackets does not change the sense the sentence makes.
Add brackets to this sentence.

The rice growing countries see Map 4 are mostly in Asia.

Understanding Year 5 Comprehension
A. Horsfield © Five Senses Education © W. Marlin

Charlotte's Web Book Cover

There are three external parts to a book – the front cover, the spine and the back cover.

The main job of a book's front cover is to encourage the reader to pick the book up. The front cover should clearly indicate what the book is about while grabbing the reader's attention and convincing her/him to read the blurb on the back cover.

The design, colour and pictures of the cover will indicate who could be interested in buying the book. The author's name is also very important when choosing a book. The spine may be the least attractive but it is often the spine the buyer sees first, as books on shelves are often presented with the spine facing the customer.

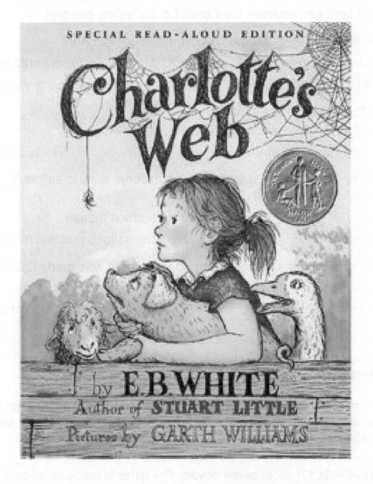

www.harpercollins.com/9780060882617/charlottes-web-read-aloud-edition

Understanding Book Covers   Circle a letter or write an answer for questions 1 to 8.

1. Who is the author of *Charlotte's Web*?

   A   Garth Williams   B   Stuart Little   C   E.B. White

2. Look at the cover picture. What has the pig's attention?

   A   a spider dropping down from a web
   B   the goose nearby making a honk sound
   C   spider webs around the writing on the book
   D   the strange look on the girl's face

3. From the cover design of *Charlotte's Web* the book would be most suitable for

   A   farmers   B   primary-aged school children
   C   teenagers   D   pest exterminators

4. After a customer picks up a book in a bookshop, that person will most likely

   A   check the back cover blurb   B   purchase the book
   C   put the book back on a shelf   D   start reading the book

5. A book cover is intended to

   A   supply work for the artist   B   explain what a book is about
   C   provide a review of the story   D   be a form of persuasion

6. The word *encourage* is made up from the prefix *en* + the word *courage*.
   What is a suitable prefix for *courage* to give it the opposite meaning to *encourage*?

   A   im   B   ex   C   dis   D   un

7. The name on the book cover is Charlotte's Web.
   Complete this sentence. (Write your answer in the box.)

   A better word than *name* for the story in a book is [   ]

8. A book is lying flat on a sale table in a bookshop.
   What is the customer **least** likely to read or check if that person is interested in the book?

   A   the cover design   B   the back cover blurb
   C   the book's author   D   the spine of the book

Lit Tip 32 – Improve your literacy skills   **The articles: a, an, the.**

In grammar, the articles are; *the, a,* and *an*. There are two types of articles.
1. The **definite** article is *the*.   2. The **indefinite** articles are *a* and *an*.
The refers to a very specific object whereas *a* and *an* refer to any object.

Can you see the difference in these? 1. A box fell off a truck. 2. The box fell off a truck.
Now try these: 3. A box fell off the truck. 4. The box fell off the truck.

Which sentence refers to a particular box falling off a particular truck? Number [   ]
Complete this sentence with the most suitable article.

I am interested in birds. I am going to buy _____ book about birds.

Understanding Year 5 Comprehension
A. Horsfield © Five Senses Education © W. Marlin

The Antique Store

Pitt's Antiques and Collectibles store looked like it was part of a collection. It was jam-packed with – junk! A window sign announced: Latest Antiques Available.

Tiana's mum headed for a dark corner of tarnished silverware. Tiana and I wandered around the shop, which was a bit of a barn. In a back corner a burly man in a black singlet was working.

Black Singlet saw us and said gruffly, 'No customers out here!'

'Wanted to speak to Mr Pitt and - ' I started.

'Youse'll find him up front!' he scowled. Tiana made a little 'Oooh!' before we retreated quickly to the shop front.

Mr Pitt put down a phone then looked up at us. He was the Mr Pitt we had seen on TV.

'We're after information. About collecting things,' I said politely. That got a frown.

'We saw you on telly,' piped in Tiana. That got a smile.

'What do people collect?' I asked.

Mr Pitt stood up tall. He pursed his lips before replying. 'No answer to that – or a million answers. People collect anything. Cars, drink cans or bottles. Teddy bears, teacups, old toys. You name it – you can collect it!'

'Does it have to be old?' I asked.

'Odd or old. If it's old you find bargains in street markets or garage sales. Trash or treasure's the name of the game. Someone's trash, another person's treasure. It's a bit late to become a numismatist or philatelist.' Another big smile.

'Coins and stamps,' muttered Tiana.

'What about, ah, . . . badges?' I suggested.

'Ephemera!' he beamed, enjoying being an expert. 'Comics too. Tossed out years ago are now worth a fortune. The trick is to start collecting things before they become popular – and dear. Get in on the ground floor.'

Understanding Narratives   Circle a letter or write an answer for questions 1 to 8.

1. The setting for the narrative is
    A   a television studio   B   a gift shop
    C   a barn   D   an antique store

2. The narrator and Tiana returned to the front of the shop to
    A   learn about collecting coins and stamps
    B   look for some antiques to buy
    C   help Tiana' mother select silverware
    D   avoid trouble with Black Singlet

3. Black Singlet uses the term *'Youse'll'*. What should he have said to be correct?
    Write your answer on the line._____

4. The sign in the window stated: *Latest Antiques Available*
    What does this imply about Mr Pitt as a businessman?
    A   he keeps up-to-date with changes
    B   he understands the importance of children
    C   he uses misleading advertising to get sales
    D   he makes every effort to satisfy customers

5. Which of the options from the text is an example of a simile?
    A   (the) store looked like it was part of a collection
    B   Tiana's mum headed for a dark corner of tarnished silverware
    C   he pursed his lips before replying
    D   someone's trash, another person's treasure

6. Which of the following would most likely be classified as an antique?
    A   a black opal   B   an ancient Chinese vase
    C   a New York baseball cap   D   a Disney movie DVD

7. Mr Pitt could best be described as being
    A   pompous   B   timid   C   jovial   D   surly

8. Mr Pitt's frown changed to a smile when he
    A   thought he was about to get a sale   B   realised he had a chance to brag
    C   saw Tiana's mother enter the store   D   was able to finish his phone call

Need to try another narrative? Check the contents page.

Lit Tip 33 – Improve your literacy skills   Punctuation in Speech

Commas in speech in text should be put in the correct place.
Look at this sentence: "Give it to Meghan," said the teacher.
The comma is after the last word spoken (*Meghan*) and before the inverted commas.
Turn the sentence around: The teacher said, "Give it to Meghan."
The comma is after said and before the inverted commas. It indicates a pause. The full stop is now included in the inverted commas.
Add the punctuation to these sentences.

1. "Time for the bus" said Dad   2. Dad said "Time for the bus "

Understanding Year 5 Comprehension
A. Horsfield © Five Senses Education © W. Marlin

How to Draw an Eiffel Tower

One of the world's most photographed landmarks, the Eiffel Tower in Paris, attracts hundreds of visitors each day. This structure might look intricate with its many lines but following these simple steps any budding artist can get a recognisable drawing.

To draw your own tower just follow these simple steps.

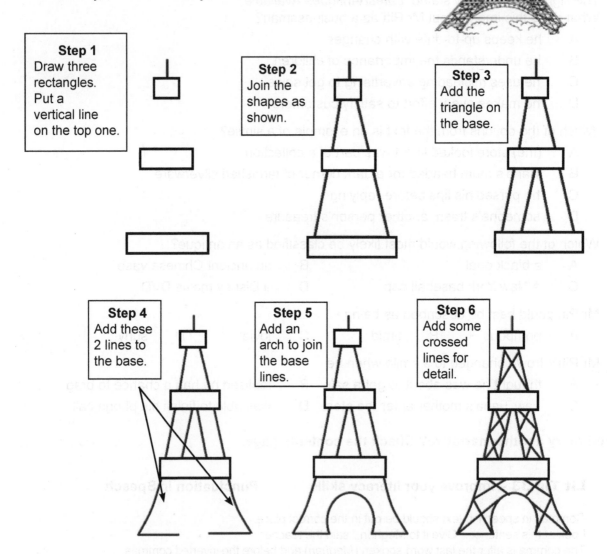

Step 1
Draw three rectangles. Put a vertical line on the top one.

Step 2
Join the shapes as shown.

Step 3
Add the triangle on the base.

Step 4
Add these 2 lines to the base.

Step 5
Add an arch to join the base lines.

Step 6
Add some crossed lines for detail.

Your tower won't have the detail of the real thing but it will look pretty good! The proportions will be realistic.

You can experiment with the additional detail as you become more confident.

Understanding Procedures

Circle a letter or write an answer for questions 1 to 8.

1. In Step 1 it is important to
- A   leave enough room on the page for the following five steps
- B   make the top vertical line long enough to take a flag
- C   have a photograph of the tower nearby to copy from
- D   get the distance between the rectangles evenly spaced

2. The Eiffel Tower is called a *landmark*? A landmark is
- A   a readily recognised feature
- B   any tall building
- C   an unacceptable structure
- D   a mark made upon the land

3. In which step is an arch included in the drawing?
- A   Step 2
- B   Step 3
- C   Step 4
- D   Step 5

4. In which city is the Eiffel Tower?

Write your answer in the box. ☐

5. The instructions would be most useful for
- A   tourists
- B   young artists
- C   photographers
- D   French people

6. What is a most likely sixth (Step 6) step for drawing an Eiffel Tower?
- A   put a flag on the top spike
- B   colour the triangle black
- C   add more structural cross lines
- D   draw a truck entering the arch

7. The text states: *any <u>budding artist</u> can get a recognisable drawing.*
A budding artist is one who
- A   has just started out as an artist
- B   shares his work with his friends
- C   needs help to develop skills
- D   is putting on weight

8. What step should a drawer of the Eiffel Tower take after adding a triangle?
- A   join the two bottom lines with a circle
- B   rub out all guide lines used when shaping the tower
- C   add lines to each end of the lowest rectangle
- D   insert many crossed lines within the tower's outline

Need to try another procedure? Check the contents page.

Lit Tip 34 – Improve your literacy skills   **Slang**

Slang refers to words that are used in casual conversation. Normally you would not use slang in important written text. It may be used in a conversation in a narrative. It can give an insight into a character.
Slang would be unacceptable when making a speech. Slang words are usually a substitution for more correct words.
Examples: grub = food, bread = money, sparkie = electrician, nerd = computer expert.
Can you work out what these slang words stand for? (Write answers in the spaces.)

lippie _____ , blowie _____ , nag _____.

An unofficial day off work (or school) is often called a s _ _ _ _ _ .

Understanding Year 5 Comprehension
A. Horsfield © Five Senses Education © W. Marlin

Water Puppets

The Thang Long Water Puppet Theatre is in Hanoi, Vietnam. It is a popular destination for domestic and foreign tourists, who want to enjoy a puppet show on and in water, and learn about Vietnamese culture and traditions through the experience.

The theatre was established in 1969. Since then many shows have been performed by the puppeteers. Every year, about 500 shows are offered to thousands of people who join the audiences. The theatre has introduced water puppetry art to more then 40 countries including Japan, France, USA, Spain and Australia through performance tours, international cultural exchange programs and puppetry festivals.

The shows are not just for children. There is something enchanting about the light-hearted comedy and intricately skilled puppetry of this troupe. Puppeteers use bamboo poles to extend their puppets from behind a back curtain and up through the surface of a shallow pond that forms the stage.

Photo: A. Horsfield

The puppeteers present brief sketches of traditional daily life of Vietnamese countryside farmers (cultivating, tending buffalo, catching fish), of community pastimes (swimming contests, dragon dancing) and ancient tales, including the historic legend of Hoan Kiem Lake and the peaceful founding of the city of Hanoi.

The Thang Long Water puppets have entertained audiences for centuries. However, the artists of Thang Long Water Puppet Theatre want to renew the old puppet shows with effects of light, music and combination between people and puppets. It sounds risky, but the theatre has been successful since its beginning and has been praised by many audiences.

Adapted from: http://www.frommers.com/destinations/hanoi/nightlife/235390#ixzz2rllqTnel

Understanding Reports   Circle a letter or write an answer for questions 1 to 8.

1. The Thang Long Water puppet plays are mainly about the
    A   way Hanoi city was founded
    B   telling stories to make people laugh
    C   everyday lives of farm workers
    D   motivation of people to work harder

2. How do the Thang Long Water puppeteers get their puppets to perform?
    A   their puppets are on long under-water bamboo poles
    B   the puppeteers swim with the puppets
    C   they stand in the pond to guide their puppets
    D   make movements in the water to keep the puppets active

3. From where in the Thang Long Water Puppet Theatre do the puppeteers operate?
    A   from positions in the front rows of the audience
    B   in front of the stage at the water's edge
    C   behind a curtain at the rear of the stage
    D   under the water's surface

4. When did the Thang Long Water Puppet Theatre begin performances?
    Write your answer in the box. ☐

5. Which statement is CORRECT according to the text?
    A   The Thang Long Water Puppets can only be seen in Hanoi.
    B   Children form the main audiences for the water puppet shows.
    C   The depth of the water on the stage is deep enough for swimming.
    D   The puppets give foreign visitors an insight into Vietnamese culture.

6. You are told the changes the Water Puppet Theatre wants to make may be risky.
    Which word is an antonym for *risky*?
    A   difficult   B   ordinary   C   costly   D   safe

7. Which is the best word to describe a group of people watching a puppet show?
    A   tourists   B   audience   C   artists   D   troupe

8. Which word in the text is used to describe a very short play?
    A   sketch   B   performance   C   entertainment   D   pastime

Need to try another report? Check the contents page.

Understanding Year 5 Comprehension
A. Horsfield © Five Senses Education © W. Marlin

Have a Safe Summer

What are UV rays? UV stands for ultraviolet. Ultraviolet light is invisible light that has an effect on the skin. Much of the UV radiation is absorbed by the ozone layer in the upper atmosphere, but dangerous amounts can pass through the ozone hole.

Sun sense

The sunlight that reaches us is made up of two types of harmful rays: long wave ultraviolet A (UVA) and short wave ultraviolet B (UVB). UVA rays can age people and UVB rays can burn people.

Sunny days are not the only days when you need UV protection. UV rays can be damaging on cool days. Check the radio UV alert, which indicates when the UV is forecast to be three or more. Use the combination of five simple sun protection measures of Slip, Slop, Slap, Seek and Slide.

Slip on sun clothing that covers as much of the skin as possible. Wear a wet suit or firm-fitting T-shirt when swimming.

Slop on water-resistant sunscreen protection Factor 30 or higher which protects against UVA and UVB rays. Apply it liberally 15 minutes before you go outdoors and top up every two hours.

Slap on a broad-rimmed hat that protects your face, head, neck and ears.

Seek shade particularly during the hours 1pm–3pm when the sun's UV rays are harshest. If this isn't possible, make sure your skin is well covered.

Slide on some UV sunglasses. Long-term exposure to UV rays can damage your eyes, so make sure you protect your eyes with high quality sunglasses.

Have a safe summer! Remember to Slip, Slop, Slap, Seek and Slide.

Sources: http://www.businessdictionary.com/definition/ultraviolet-UV-rays.html#ixzz2weAfgZFg:

foodauthority.nsw.gov.au: foodsafety asn. au: health.gov.au: Health matters NSW Teachers' Health Fund. edition 1
2014

Understanding Reports

Circle a letter to answer questions 1 to 8.

1. If a person is venturing into the sunshine for a long period they should apply sunscreen
   A   once only, 15 minutes before going into the sunshine
   B   every fifteen minutes whenever they are in a sunny place
   C   every thirty minutes while in direct sunlight
   D   after the first application every two hours of sunlight

2. The instruction to **SLAP** is an instruction to
   A   put on a broad-rimmed hat   B   put on sunglasses
   C   wear a wet suit   D   apply a suitable sunscreen

3. According to the text the difference between UVA rays and UVB rays is their
   A   safety level   B   wavelength   C   speed   D   colour

4. The words '**slip, slop, slap**' are an example of
   A   onomatopoeia   B   rhyme   C   homophones   D   alliteration
       (see **Lit Tip 23**)   (see **Lit Tip 16**)   (see **Lit Tip 24**)

5. According to the text some people may believe that
   A   UVA rays do not harm young people
   B   it is easy to see the difference between UVA rays and UVB rays
   C   there is no need for sun protection on cool days
   D   the ozone absorbs all dangerous UV rays

6. To find the UV level each day a person can
   A   check to see if the sky is blue   B   watch the daily temperature predictions
   C   look for a hole in the ozone   D   listen to radio weather reports

7. The source of UV rays is the
   A   sun   B   ozone hole   C   atmosphere   D   ozone layer

8. It is advised in the text that the sunscreen should be
   A   skin colour   B   water resistant
   C   used sparingly   D   less than Factor 30

Need to try another report? Check the contents page.

Lit Tip 36 – Improve your Literacy skills   **Prefixes for numbers**

A prefix can give a clue to useful numbers. An <u>oct</u>agon has eight sides. An <u>oct</u>opus has eight arms. Octa and octo indicate eight (8).

The prefixes mono and uni refer to one (1). A <u>uni</u>cycle has one wheel. A <u>mono</u>rail is a single rail usually suspended above the ground.

Bi means two (2). A <u>bi</u>cycle has two wheels. A <u>bi</u>plane has two wings.

Tri mean three (3). A <u>tri</u>angle is three sided. <u>Tri</u>ple means three times as many.

Quad means four (4). A <u>quad</u>rilateral has four sides. A <u>quad</u>-bike has four wheels.

How many legs on a tripod? _____   How many horns does a unicorn have? _____

Understanding Year 5 Comprehension
A. Horsfield © Five Senses Education © W. Marlin

Pro Hart: an Outback Legend

Pro Hart lived most of his life around Broken Hill (NSW). He painted almost every day of his life but was not always well accepted among fellow artists.

Pro Hart was born in Broken Hill, in 1928. His early years were spent on "Larloona" a sheep station, 130km from Broken Hill. He was educated at home through the correspondence school. By age seven he was illustrating his schoolwork and steadily developing his talent.

He returned to Broken Hill in his early twenties where he continued to paint and draw when not working long underground shifts in a mine. The hard work and the miners provided much inspiration for his paintings. Pro took art classes to his improve his techniques.

He was married in 1960.

Pro was 'discovered' by an Adelaide gallery owner in 1962.

His popularity as an outback artist began to climb.

Collection after collection would sell out and Pro began travelling the world. His art hangs in large international collections. He met and was admired by princes, presidents and movie stars, but the shy man preferred the company of his mates.

Mainly working in oils and acrylics, Pro experimented with art techniques all his life - dropping paint from hot air balloons, creating ice sculptures and even using a cannon to spread paint on his chosen surface. Perhaps his most famous moment came with a series of television carpet commercials.

Pro was also a sculptor working with welded steel, bronze and ceramics.

In 1976 he was awarded an MBE for his services to art in Australia. In 1983 he received an Australian Citizen of the Year Award. He died in 2006 at his home in Broken Hill.

Understanding Recounts   Circle a letter or write an answer for questions 1 to 8.

1. A biography is a
    A   written recount of a person's life
    B   record of a person's achievements
    C   story of a person's life written by that person
    D   fictional narrative written to impress readers

2. When did Pro Hart receive his Australian Citizen of the Year Award?
    A   1962   B   1976   C   1983   D   2006

3. Pro Hart is described as a legend. In this text it means he was
    A   regarded highly as an artist   B   the subject of a folk tale
    C   a man with mystical powers   D   said to have super powers

4. Where did Pro Hart spend most of his life?
    A   Adelaide   B   Broken Hill
    C   Larloona sheep station   D   mining underground

5. Write the numbers 1 to 4 in the boxes to show the correct order in which events occurred in the
   recount. The first one (1) has been done for you.

	Pro Hart worked on a sheep station
	Pro Hart awarded at MBE
	Pro Hart got married
1	Pro Hart was born in Broken Hill

6. Pro Hart first became involved in art when he
    A   worked in the mines   B   made TV commercials
    C   visited the Adelaide art gallery D   was a correspondence school pupil

7. Which word best describes Pro Hart?
    A   sociable   B   shy   C   brash   D   conventional

8. Other than painting what other artistic interest did Pro Hart have?
    A   ballooning   B   shooting   C   sculpture   D   fashion

Need to try another recount? Check the contents page.

Lit Tip 37 – Improve your literacy skills   Interjections

<u>Hey</u>! Get off my lawn. In this text *Hey* is called an interjection.

Interjections are small words or sounds. Mostly they are short exclamations, such as *Hmm, Yuk!* and *Whoa!* They can express strong sudden emotion, surprise, joy and enthusiasm. They are often used to attract attention.

They are mostly at or before the start of a sentence.

An interjection is not related to any other part of speech, such as nouns and verbs.
Interjection examples: Indeed!, Well!, Hear, hear!, Yep!, Phew!, Oops, Eek

Sometimes vulgar words are used as interjections. Do not use them in your writing!
Underline the best interjection to complete these sentences.

1. (Wow! Hmm)That's good!   2. (Gosh, Yippee!) I'm tired.   3. (What! Hi) It's wrong!

Understanding Year 5 Comprehension
A. Horsfield © Five Senses Education © W. Marlin

Bosley

Bosley was getting fed up with his home.
The food was an utter disgrace.
They fed him with fish that came out of a tin
Of a quality really just fit for the bin.
And he knew he was getting decidedly thin.
So he set out to find a new place.

He followed his nose to a Sea Food café
That sent him right into a spin.
For the smells that were wafting from inside the door,
Guaranteed that some wonderful meals were in store.
And the growl in his stomach became a loud roar!
So he opened the door and went in.

Now the cook was a man with a very soft heart
And he couldn't turn Bosley away.
So he gave him a meal on his very own dish
Full of oysters and prawns and the best kind of fish.
A feast that a gourmet like Bosley would wish.
With the promise of more the next day.

But back at his home things were really quite grim
For his owners were missing their pet.
And they'd printed up posters to put round the street
With a picture of Bosley, angelic and sweet.
And a promise to serve him the very best meat
If he'd only forgive and forget.

So Bosley the cat now has visiting rights
At the Sea Food Café up the way.
'Though he spends winter nights on a rug by the fire
And his owners give in to his every desire,
He can often be seen strolling up to inquire
What the café is serving today.

Elaine Horsfield

Understanding Poetry

Circle a letter or write an answer for questions 1 to 8.

1. Bosley left home because
    A   he was invited to eat at a Sea Food Café
    B   the food he was given was not nice
    C   he had to sleep on a rug
    D   his owners didn't feed him

2. According to the text how did Bosley's owners go about getting him to return home?
    A   they stopped the cook at the Sea Food Café from feeding him
    B   they gave him his own special plate for meals
    C   they collected him from the Sea Food Café
    D   they put up posters pleading for his return

3. Which text from the poem is an example of alliteration? (see Lit Tip 24)
    A   forgive and forget   B   rug by the fire
    C   angelic and sweet   D   the best kind of fish

4. The first stanza of the poem mainly explains why Bosley was
    A   unloved   B   a scavenger   C   thin   D   a fish eater

5. The poet uses these words in the third stanza:
    the cook was a man with a very soft heart
    By saying the cook has a soft heart the poet is implying he
    A   felt pity towards Bosley   B   was easily upset by neglect
    C   had a heart problem   D   did not exercise enough

6. For Bosley, which word best describes how he felt about his owners?
    They were
    A   cruel   B   neglectful   C   attentive   D   thoughtless

7. Which word from stanza 4 rhymes with pet?
    A   grim   B   forget   C   sweet   D   cat

8. Bosley was fed from a dish like this one at the Sea Food Café.
    Is this statement TRUE or FALSE? (Tick a box.)

    TRUE ☐   FALSE ☐

Need to try another poem? Check the contents page.

Lit Tip 38 – Improve your literacy skills   Paired nouns

Some names are two words joined by and. Oranges and lemons is the name of a song.
Oranges and lemons is treated as a single noun. It should be used with a single verb
(see Lit Tip 8).
Other paired examples include fish and chips and Jack and Jill (the nursery rhyme).

Underline the correct verbs to complete these sentences.
1. Rock and roll (is, are) dance music.   2. Rum and Coke (is, are) an alcoholic drink.
3. Anthony and Cleopatra (was, were) written by Shakespeare.

Understanding Year 5 Comprehension
A. Horsfield © Five Senses Education © W. Marlin

The World's Longest Cliffs

At almost 400 kilometres in length the Bunda Cliffs and Baxter Cliffs at the edge of the Nullarbor Plain, are part of the Great Australian Bight. They are the world's longest cliff face. The Bunda Cliffs is an aboriginal name which is used in South Australia for the name of the Nullarbor coastal cliffs.

The Great Australian Bight is a bend in the coastline - an open bay. It is the world's largest indentation, about 1,150 km consisting of many long cliffs and some beaches. The cliffs along the Great Australian Bight run as high as 60 m to 120 m, bordering the Nullarbor Plain.

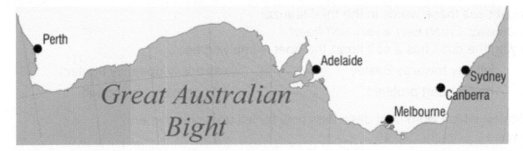

The Great Australian Bight starts in Western Australia and stretches all the way to Victoria. While Europeans didn't explore the shores of the Bight until the 19th century, the area has been_____(8)_____by Aboriginal people for tens of thousands of years.

The Nullarbor Plain is a sparsely populated area of South Australia. It is extremely dry with very little surface water. It can now be crossed using the Eyre Highway, named after the famed explorer Edward John Eyre. Eyre was the first European explorer to survive a gruelling East-West crossing of Australia in the mid-1800s.

Even in his distressed condition as he explored his way across the Nullarbor, Eyre was impressed by the cliffs. In his journal he wrote: "Distressing and fatal as these cliffs might prove to us, there was a grandeur in their appearance that was most imposing, and which struck me with admiration. Stretching out before us in unbroken line… and glittering in the morning sun which had now risen upon them, and made the scene beautiful even amidst the dangers and anxieties of our situation."

Source: http://thelongestlistofthelongeststuffatthelongestdomainnameatlonglast.com/long334.html

Understanding Reports   Circle a letter to answer questions 1 to 8.

1. What is a bight?
   - A   It is a stretch of open ocean.
   - B   It is a long line of cliffs.
   - C   It is where the ocean meets the land.
   - D   It is a curve in the coastline.

2. How long is the Great Australian Bight?
   - A   60 km
   - B   120 km
   - C   400 km
   - D   1,150 km

3. How many states does the Great Australian Bight stretch across?
   - A   one
   - B   two
   - C   three
   - D   four

4. Not many people live on the Nullarbor Plain because
   - A   there is little water there
   - B   the land is very flat
   - C   the Bunda cliffs are dangerous
   - D   it is a long way from Victoria

5. According to the text which statement is CORRECT?
   - A   The Bunda cliffs run from Perth to Adelaide.
   - B   Edward John Eyre designed the Eyre Highway across the Nullarbor.
   - C   The Aboriginal people have lived on the Nullarbor Plain for centuries.
   - D   The coast along the Great Australian Bight is an unbroken line of cliffs.

6. How did Edward John Eyre react when he saw the Bunda Cliffs?
   He was
   - A   distressed
   - B   awed
   - C   anxious
   - D   unimpressed

7. Choose the word from the text that begins with a prefix.
   - A   across
   - B   singular
   - C   populated
   - D   largest

8. A word has been deleted from the text.
   Which word would be best suited to the space (8)?
   - A   studied
   - B   developed
   - C   occupied
   - D   farmed

Need to try another report? Check the contents page.

Understanding Year 5 Comprehension
A. Horsfield © Five Senses Education © W. Marlin

Yuri's New School

'Morning class. We have a new student at Towambin today,' Mr Bell said after the class had settled down. 'This is Yuri. Yuri will be with us for a few weeks. I want you to treat him in the friendly way we all treat each other at Towambin.'

Yuri was sitting in a seat by himself near the middle of the room.

'Is Yuri really your name?' someone behind Yuri asked.

'Yes, Yuri is his name. Yuri Kirokov.' Mr Bell was quite definite.

'Sounds like a cough!' someone called softly, then did an imitation of a coughing sound. 'Kiro-cough! Got a bad throat.'

'It's not the only thing you'll have Tom if you keep that up!' said Mr Bell, not unkindly.

'His dad works on our farm. He's picking beans,' someone volunteered.

'Thank you Debbie, I'm sure Yuri will tell us all about himself as he gets to know us.'

'Can he speak English?' a girl asked as she raised her hand.

Mr Bell raised his eyes to the ceiling. 'Christine, I will let you work that out.'

'Does he have to wear our school uniform, Sir?' a boy called from the back of the room.

'No, he doesn't. He might only be here a few weeks. Enough questions. We need to make a start.'

Underneath the noise of getting out books someone muttered that it wasn't fair.

For the rest of the day Yuri worked quietly. Not asking questions, not volunteering answers, but always ready with a good answer when asked.

In the grounds he kept to himself. He watched the other kids play from a bench under a tree.

Most children were friendly or disinterested. They all had their own friends. Played their own games.

A couple made soft coughing noises when they came near. There's always one, Yuri thought. There was a slight pain in his stomach. It was the first time since leaving City Rd School.

Understanding Narratives

Circle a letter to answer questions 1 to 8.

1. Where is the Towambin School most likely situated?
   - A   in a farming district
   - B   near City Rd School
   - C   in a large suburb
   - D   near a medical clinic

2. Who pretended to have a bad cough?
   - A   Yuri
   - B   Debbie
   - C   Christine
   - D   Tom

3. During his first day at Towambin School Yuri
   - A   mixed with other students
   - B   kept much to himself
   - C   was cheeky in class
   - D   didn't understand the work

4. You read: *Mr Bell raised his eyes to the ceiling.*
   When Mr Bell raised his eyes like this he was
   - A   showing light-hearted disbelief
   - B   trying to control his temper
   - C   wondering if he knew the answer
   - D   thinking about what to do next

5. Yuri didn't have to wear Towambin School uniform. Why was this?
   - A   No other students had to wear a school uniform.
   - B   He still had his City Rd School uniform.
   - C   He was not a permanent Towambin student.
   - D   His father hadn't been paid for his work.

6. The students at Towambin School who pretended to be coughing were trying to
   - A   become friends with Yuri
   - B   make Yuri laugh
   - C   compel Yuri to leave the school
   - D   provoke Yuri to react

7. The word *volunteered*, as used in the text means the information was
   - A   requested by the teacher
   - B   offered freely and openly
   - C   already known by the students
   - D   not necessarily correct

8. Another suitable title for the passage would be
   - A   First Day
   - B   Kid with a cough
   - C   Mr Bell's class
   - D   School uniforms

Need to try another narrative? Check the contents page.

Lit Tip 40 – Improve your Literacy skills   **Poor story beginnings**

The opening few sentences of a story are important. The reader will often decide whether or not to keep reading from these words.
Don't tell too much in the beginning of your story. You want the reader to be interested enough to want to read on and find out more!
Some poor opening sentences: Once upon a time
                                              The night was dark and stormy
OR something like this: My name is (insert your name) I am a (boy/girl) and I am (insert age) years old and I live (insert place) with (insert other people).
There is too much nninteresting and useless information for the start of a great story!

Understanding Year 5 Comprehension
A. Horsfield © Five Senses Education © W. Marlin

SOLUTIONS

ANSWERS – Reading Comprehension Tests   84, 85

ANSWERS – Literacy Tip Exercises   86, 87

Understanding Year 5 Comprehension
A. Horsfield © Five Senses Education © W. Marlin

No.   Title   Answers

1. Those Poor Plants: 1. B   2. C   3. C   4. D   5. D   6. C   7. A   8. A

2. The City Dump: 1. B   2. C   3. plums   4. A   5. D   6. C   7. B   8. D

3. Christmas Lights: 1. D   2. B   3. A   4. B   5. C   6. D   7. B   8. A

4. What is a Hammer? 1. A   2. C   3. B   4. D   5. C   6. B   7. club hammer   8. A

5. The Curtain Fig: 1. D   2. D   3. A   4. D   5. B   6. C   7. NO   8. B

6. A Japanese Folk Tale: 1. C   2. C   3. A   4. B   5. A   6. C   7. A   8. D

7. Sugar Cane Milling: 1. C   2. B   3. A   4. D   5. juice   6. C   7. B   8. D

8. Climb on Board: 1. C   2. A   3. D   4. B   5. (2, 4, 1, 3)   6. C   7. B   8. A

9. Ice Cream Van Flier: 1. C   2. B   3. A   4. D   5. C   6. B   7. D   8. A

10. What are Verbs? 1. D   2. A   3. B   4. ate   5. C   6. D   7. A   8. C

11. Dogs in Cars: 1. A   2. C   3. D   4. B   5. A   6. B   7. C   8. D

12. What Will You Be? 1. A   2. C   3. D   4. B   5. C   6. A   7. C   8. Toad

13. The Skateboard: 1. C   2. D   3. B   4. D   5. C   6. exclaimed, added, declared   7. A   8. A

14. What is a Quandong? 1. B   2. A   3. D   4. D   5. C   6. A   7. C   8. B

15. Precious Gold: 1. C   2. B   3. A   4. B   5. A   6. D   7. silver OR nickel   8. B

16. Bat-winged Cannibal Fly: 1. A   2. two wings   3. B   4. D   5. A   6. False   7. B   8. C

17. Gone Phishing: 1. B   2. C   3. Example: phone   4. C   5. A   6. D   7. B   8. A

18. The Final Kombi: 1. 63   2. A   3. B   4. C   5. B   6. D   7. C   8. A

19. The Microbe: 1. A   2. C   3. D   4. B   5. C   6. B   7. D   8. A

20. Origin of Tea: 1. A   2. B   3. Szechwan   4. A   5. C   6. B   7. B   8. D

Continued on the next page...

No.	Title	Answers

No.   Title   Answers

21. Redundancies: 1. B   2. D   3. A   4. C   5. B   6. B   7. D   8. A

22. Christmas Lights: 1. A   2. D   3. D   4. C   5. B   6. D   7. B   8. C

23. How to Whistle: 1. A   2. D   3. B   4. C   5. (2, 4, 1, 3)   6. A   7. B   8. B

24. Tokaanu Thermal Walk: 1. A   2. C   3. B   4. D   5. A   6. B   7. D   8. B

25. Where in Australia? 1. D   2. Patterson   3. A   4. C   5. B   6. C   7. B   8. A

26. The Fly Trap: 1. D   2. B   3. A   4. A   5. D   6. A   7. C   8. B

27. Comic Strips: 1. 4   2. A   3. C   4. D   5. B   6. D   7. C   8. A

28. Summer Fun: 1. D   2. C   3. A   4. B   5. D   6. C   7. B   8. A

29. The Humble Spade: 1. B   2. C   3. Factual   4. D   5. B   6. A   7. C   8. D

30. Letter to an Editor: 1. C   2. B   3. A   4. B   5. D   6. A   7. C   8. D

31. Land Sailing: 1. B   2. D   3. C   4. A   5. C   6. D   7. B   8. D

32. Book Cover: 1. C   2. A   3. B   4. A   5. D   6. C   7. title   8. D

33. The Antique Store: 1. D   2. D   3. you will (OR you'll)   4. C   5. A   6. B   7. A   8. B

34. How to draw an Eiffel Tower: 1. D   2. A   3. D   4. Paris   5. B   6. C   7. A   8. C

35. Water Puppets: 1. C   2. A   3. C   4. 1969   5. D   6. D   7. B   8. A

36. Have a Safe Summer: 1. D   2. A   3. B   4. D   5. C   6. D   7. A   8. B

37. Pro Hart: an Outback Legend: 1. A   2. C   3. A   4. B   5. (2, 4, 3, 1)   6. D   7. B   8. C

38. Bosley: 1. B   2. D   3. A   4. C   5. A   6. D   7. B   8. False

39. The World's Longest Cliffs: 1. D   2. D   3. C   4. A   5. C   6. B   7. A   8. C

40. Yuri's New School: 1. A   2. D   3. B   4. A   5. C   6. D   7. B   8. A

Understanding Year 5 Comprehension
A. Horsfield © Five Senses Education © W. Marlin

Year 5 Answers

Lit Tips Exercises

No. Text title	Topic	Answers
1. Those Poor Plants: stated	Better words than *said*	Examples: chirped, growled,
2. The City Dump:	Unusual plurals	geese, wolves, salmon, women, cacti, media
3. Christmas Lights 1:	Phrases	1. on the hill, 2. under the bush, 3. by the fence, 4. near the step
4. What is a Hammer?	The suffix *ess*	tigress, empress, duchess, countess
5. The Curtain Fig:	Triple compound words	altogether, motherhood, potatoes
6. Tsunami Folk Tale :	Similes and Clichés	Example: as fluffy as a pompom
7. Sugar Cane Milling:	Gender	masculine, masculine, feminine, common, neuter OR: M, M, F, C, N
8. Climb on Board:	Singular verbs	Examples: plays, grows, runs, hurts
9. Ice Cream Van Flier:	The prefix *pre*	A 4, B 1, C 2, D 3
10. What are Verbs?	Tense	present, past, future, thought
11. Dogs in Cars:	Apostrophes for plurals	mice's, girls' women's
12. What Will You Be?	Being precise	Examples: 1. stared/glared, 2. peered
13. The Skateboard:	Metaphors	Examples 1, 3 and 4
14. What is a Quandong?:	Collective nouns	the gang . . . robs
15. Precious Gold:	Abstract nouns	1. hope, faith, talent, 2. beauty
16. Bat-winged Cannibal Fly:	Homophones	hare, maid, write, tale
17. Gone Phishing:	Question marks	Oral responses
18. The Final Kombi:	Analogies	gates (to gardens)
19. The Microbe:	Possessive pronouns	Examples: 1. his, 2. mine
20. Origin of Tea:	Being precise	Examples: nibbled, gnawed, gobbled

Continued on the next page...

No. Text title	Topic	Answers
21. Redundancies:	s endings for singular nouns	Examples: was, is, was, is
22. Christmas Lights 2:	Word building	Examples: knows, known, unknown knowledge, knowing, acknowledge
23. How to Whistle:	Onomatopoeia	Examples: tinkle, boom
24. Tokaanu Thermal Walk:	Alliteration	1. m 2. tw 3. fi Examples: Ben, Tammy, Peter, Henry
25. Where in Australia?	Comparing adjectives	newer, newest: more interesting, most interesting
26. Venus Fly Trap:	Euphemisms	used/second hand, died
27. Comic Strips:	Writing addresses	Individual responses
28. Summer Fun:	Non-sentences	No response required
29. The Humble Spade:	The prefixe *a*	afloat, alive, ashore
30. Letter to an Editor:	Persuasive text words	No response required
31. Land Sailing:	Brackets	(see Map 4)
32. Book Cover:	Articles: *a, an, the*	4 (The box fell off the truck.), a
33. The Antique Store:	Punctuation in speech	1. "Time for the bus," said Dad. 2. Dad said, "Time for the bus."
34. Draw an Eiffel Tower:	Slang	lipstick, blowfly, horse, sickie
35. Water Puppets:	Legends, myths and other tales	Once upon a time
36. Have a Safe Summer:	Prefixes for numbers	three (3) legs, one (1) horn
37. Pro Hart:	Interjections	1. Wow, 2. Gosh, 3. What
38. Bosley:	Paired nouns	1. is, 2. is, 3. was
39. World's Longest Cliffs:	Using indefinite articles	a yak, a unicorn, an idiot, a united team, an unhappy prince
40. Yuri's New School:	Poor story beginnings	No response required.

Understanding Year 5 Comprehension
A. Horsfield © Five Senses Education © W. Marlin

Notes